GRAVEL RIDES
SCOTLAND

GRAVEL RIDES SCOTLAND

**28 gravel bike
adventures in
the wilds of
Scotland**

ED SHOOTE

Vertebrate Publishing, Sheffield
www.adventurebooks.com

GRAVEL RIDES SCOTLAND
28 gravel bike adventures in the wilds of Scotland
ED SHOOTE

VP First published in 2022 by Vertebrate Publishing. Reprinted in 2022 and 2023.

Vertebrate Publishing, Omega Court, 352 Cemetery Road, Sheffield S11 8FT, United Kingdom.
www.adventurebooks.com

Front cover *The northern end of Loch Shiel (route 24).*
Back cover (L–R) *The Kinesis Tripster ATR in its natural environment looking towards the Balmoral Estate (route 17);*
The long gravel stretch alongside Loch Ericht (route 20); Fantastic gravel riding in the shadow of Lochnagar (route 17);
The river crossing at the upper end of Glen Quoich – not one for wet weather (route 16).
Opposite *Bikepacking just south of Fort William.*
Photography by **Ed Shoote** unless otherwise credited.

Mapping contains data from OS © Crown copyright and database right (2022) and © OpenStreetMap contributors,
Openstreetmap.org/copyright
Relief shading produced from data derived from U.S. Geological Survey, National Geospatial Program.
Cartography by Richard Ross, Active Maps Ltd. – **www.activemaps.co.uk**

Edited by Helen Parry, design by Jane Beagley, layout and production by Cameron Bonser, Vertebrate Publishing.

Printed and bound in China by Latitude Press.

Vertebrate Publishing is committed to printing on paper from sustainable sources.

MIX
Paper | Supporting
responsible forestry
FSC® C010256
www.fsc.org

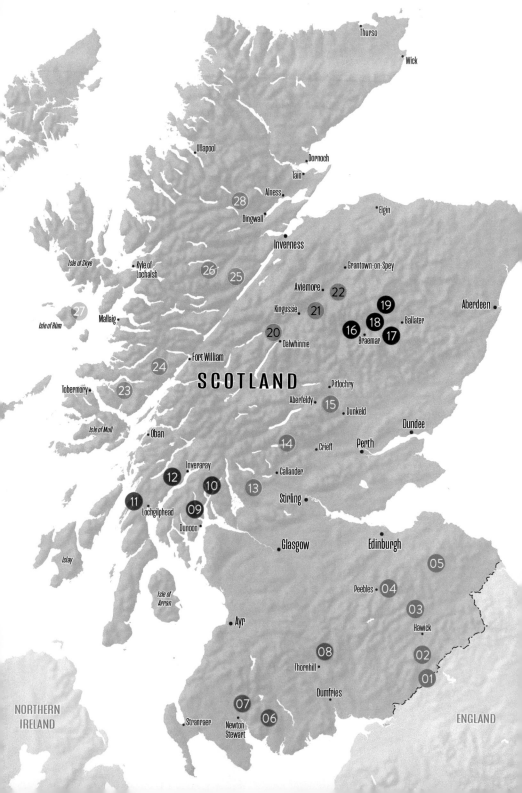

CONTENTS

Download the
Gravel Rides Scotland
GPX files from
www.adventurebooks.com/
GRS-GPX

Introduction

The word 'gravel' is likely to be of Celtic origin, which is appropriate because Scotland is certainly one of the best places to ride bikes on gravel.

I have ridden bikes in many amazing places all around the world, but I am lucky to call Scotland my home and it has been an amazing experience to explore its hidden corners while putting this book together.

Despite Scotland's amazing gravel cycling, my love of this type of riding began a long time ago when living in Canada. I took a Kona-branded Jake the Snake cyclo-cross bike, fitted the widest tyres I could, then explored endless miles of gravel logging roads, deep into the British Columbia wilderness. I loved getting lost in such beautiful places, but there were just a few too many grizzly bear encounters for comfort. What really sealed my love of gravel riding was being lent one of the very first Kinesis Tripster ATR (adventure, tour, race) bikes for a big trip. This bike was so comfortable on longer rides I rode it heading east all the way to Istanbul twice and then on to China and beyond, taking in a lot of gravel tracks on the way. Back in Scotland, I became obsessed with exploring the glens, mountains and forests by gravel bike.

This book is intended to be a collection of adventure rides that fit my take on the modern genre of gravel bikes. I have always had a love of 'type 2 fun' when riding; this is a sense of wanting to ride further and higher which I think is reflected in these routes. Don't let this put you off because it is these challenges that you'll remember the best.

I wanted to focus on Scotland as it has so much riding and is one of the best places in the world to ride gravel bikes. Not only does it have stunning scenery but unlike other parts of the UK you are not limited to a few rights of way; the Scottish Outdoor Access Code (SOAC) essentially means that if you see a track in the hills and it is *responsible*, *safe* and *sustainable*

to ride it, then you can usually do so (save for certain exemptions). There are many off-road tracks in Scotland, built for many reasons – from military roads in the eighteenth century through to constructing wind farms in the twenty-first century. From stalking paths on Highland estates to private roads heading to ruined cottages and castles, each trail has a story and hopefully this book tells a few and answers some questions you might find yourself asking along the way.

With so many gravel options in Scotland it can be hard to know where to start, so this book showcases seven of the very best gravelling regions in the country. It focuses on areas that are perfect for weekends away or linking longer routes together for bikepacking. Partly these clusters are an environmental consideration so you can stay in one location for a few days and reduce your driving. Quite a few of the routes are accessible by train; the book indicates if there is a train station nearby and also suggests ways to use the train to access some great linear rides.

Enjoy this book and the adventures it will inspire – there will be hard climbs and long days but there will also be perfect gravel descents, well-deserved cafe stops, quick dips in a loch on a sunny day and an abundance of fresh air (and rain) in your face. Ride faster, ride further and ride gravel.

OPPOSITE PLAYING ON THE BEACH NEAR GATEHOUSE OF FLEET.

Acknowledgements

I would like to thank my wife Marion for tolerating the weekends away 'researching' and my children, Orrin and Alana, for accompanying me on some routes in seats and trailers. Huge thanks to Rory and the team at Kinesis bikes for all the support since my first crazy trip in 2014 – the Tripster ATR is what really gave me the gravel bug. Thanks to Gore Wear and Apidura for supporting me with kit that lets me get out in any weather. Thanks to Rachel Botterill for making the connections to give me the opportunity to write this book. Thanks to Graeme and the team at Developing Mountain Biking in Scotland for everything they have helped with and tolerated about gravel. Finally, thanks to all those putting together so many new routes inspiring riders in Scotland – there's too many to mention without missing one, but it's great to see.

Gravel riding

Gravel riding has become a real movement within cycling; however, to understand the context for this book it's best to strip it back and consider that gravel is just the predominant surface type on a bike ride. Gravel mostly means tracks but also smooth paths, singletrack and quiet roads too. Gravel riding isn't just easy mountain biking, it's about exploring off-road further and faster than you would on a mountain bike.

Modern gravel bikes roll fast and, with drop handlebars, they let you cover longer distances and still enjoy road sections too. For this reason, gravel routes may include longer road sections than those on a traditional mountain bike ride.

It is true that cyclists have ridden on gravel tracks ever since the first bike was invented and 'gravel riding' is just a relatively new term for something that already existed – some cynics say it's just a marketers' dream. However, what it has already achieved in inspiring riders to explore or re-engage with cycling is amazing.

Gravel riding is about accessible riding; gravel bikes get more people out riding and enjoying adventures away from cars and from their own doorstep on a daily basis. This book offers seven outstanding gravel destinations to visit across Scotland, so you can stay a while and explore each. The perfect gravel route is different for different riders; most of the routes are flexible, being very easily shortened or lengthened, while options to include or cut out technical riding are described to tailor the adventure for all riders.

Why is gravel riding booming?

Gravel riding bridges the great divide in cycling between roadies and mountain bikers. For mountain bikers, gravel bikes let you explore further than you might on the chunky tyres of a mountain bike. For road riders, gravel tracks let you explore and open up adventures away from the monotony and ever more busy traffic on roads. Finally, gravel riding is the perfect introduction to cycling for beginners too, because it is straightforward and easily accessible. Combine all this and you start to see why gravel riding is already a huge part of cycling culture.

While riding gravel tracks has always been part of off-road biking, modern dedicated gravel bikes are faster and more capable than ever before. Some of the route sections in this book were previously seen as classic mountain bike routes. However, as gravel riding has evolved, these sections are now being used as parts of longer gravel routes.

Where did gravel riding suddenly come from?

Gravel riding's popularity was kick started by a number of things. More and more riders were looking for adventure bikes capable of exploring remote areas on rougher tracks faster than traditional touring bikes ever could. In the last decade the sport of gravel racing started booming in North America, while in the UK awareness of

Map key

Route line

Shortcut/
optional route lines

S Start

3 Route marker

06a Optional route

Route direction

gravel riding grew thanks to events like the Dirty Reiver. The result has been bikes that take wider tyres for comfort and grip and are designed to be more comfortable and versatile than a cyclo-cross or road bike, while still being fast. The Covid-19 pandemic led to unprecedented numbers of gravel bikes being sold, undoubtedly because riders were forced to stay local and discovered the buzz of exploring new trails on their doorstep that they never knew existed. As a result of the versatility of gravel bikes, people have realised that they maybe don't need both a mountain bike *and* a road bike and that they can settle on just one bike.

Gravel bikes

An ideal bike for these routes would have the following features:
- 40–55-millimetre tyre width, in either 700c or 650b.
- Tubeless tyres (these are required due to the rough nature of these routes), meaning lower pressures are needed and small punctures will self-seal.
- A range of gears that go below a 1:1 ratio (this means a smaller ring on the front than the back) to help on the frequent steep and long climbs.
- Hydraulic disc brakes (meaning you have more control on the descents when on drop bars; another advantage being that they require a lot less maintenance compared to cable operated brakes).

Gravel handlebars are a personal choice – flared, drop handlebars are the most popular option on gravel bikes as they offer more control off-road and can be more forgiving too. It's also worth considering some sort of suspension (either a vibration damping frame, stem, or bars; a suspension fork; or a hardtail front suspension mountain bike).

Shorter gravel routes are great for family riding; quite a few of the routes were researched with a child trailer or child seat in tow. A seat or trailer with suspension of some form is recommended. Gravel bikes improve the riding experience by making it easier to cover longer distances, but realistically any old mountain bike will get you around. To use an old cliché: the best bike is the bike you already have, so long as it is reliable and suitable for riding off-road.

How to use this book

Route grading

Routes are graded using a gravel scale which incorporates the roughness or technicality of the gravel and riding – essentially rating 1 for smooth and well surfaced through to 5 for rocky or poorly surfaced with mud. This gravel scale is based on the author's judgement and considers the route as a whole, rather than just reflecting the hardest part of the route.

Gravel scale

 1 Well-surfaced fine, smooth gravel or quiet back roads.

 2 Slightly coarse gravel sections; may include sections of narrow but smooth singletrack.

 3 Longer sections of coarser gravel or short sections of rocky tracks. Very short sections of mud that can be soft in the wet. Short sections of singletrack that might be bumpy in places.

 4 Gravel is mostly coarse; longer sections of rocky track that may require a short push. Singletrack sections may be natural and rougher than built gravel paths.

 5 A large part of the route is on very rough, rocky tracks; some longer pushes required. May include longer sections of singletrack which is bumpy and muddy and might be very narrow too. Not for inexperienced riders as a good level of skill is required. Crossing into mountain biking terrain.

This gravel scale does not factor in the physical challenge of a route – this is indicated by the statistics on length and metres of ascent. Together with the gravel scale, this information should give you a good idea of the time expected to ride it. Any specific considerations like steep climbs or sections off the bike will also be noted separately in the route details. All this information should give a good overview of whether the route is within your ability.

The routes in this book contain just about every style of gravel possible; they are chosen to suit a range of rider preferences from beginners looking for smooth tracks to mountain bikers looking to 'underbike' by taking a gravel bike on techy sections. All the routes are rideable by gravel bike and within the entire book there are only a handful of hike-a-bikes (an off-the-bike carry or push), be it a very steep climb for only the strongest legs or a muddy path to connect a wonderful complete circuit. In these cases, the route is so good it is worth including despite the disadvantage of a hike-a-bike section.

Navigation, accuracy and route conditions

Directions are provided for each route. These highlight any tricky sections or potential navigational issues; the route overview provides a useful outline of the conditions and types of surface you'll encounter. There is also an interesting section on the local area, to provide some context and background information.

The GPX files provided (see page vii) can be easily uploaded on to a GPS device or smartphone to aid with navigation. GPS is usually reliable and accurate, but taking a paper map and compass and knowing how to use them is strongly recommended. Ordnance Survey (OS) maps are most commonly used and are available as a mobile app; the route information specifies the 1:50,000-scale OS Landranger maps needed for the routes. This scale of map is the most practical option to pack in your bag;

however, at this scale some tracks are missing or marked as paths. New gravel track development in Scotland is happening at pace so bear in mind that very recent forest or wind farm tracks may not be on your map, or even on some digital GPS mapping yet. Uniform plantation forests or wind farms can be confusing and disorientating. It is noted in the route descriptions when navigation becomes particularly challenging; a compass (or GPS) can help greatly.

While every effort has been made to ensure accuracy within the directions and descriptions in this book, things change and we are unable to guarantee that every detail will be correct. The route conditions might have changed – a large storm can wash out roads or destroy river crossings – while forestry works can churn up large sections of track, making progress much slower than expected. Occasionally routes used for construction get decommissioned or even dug up. For this reason, the routes in this book are guides only and must be planned and ridden with prudence. Please treat stated distance and elevation as guidelines and exercise caution if part of a GPX file or some information in the text appears at odds with the route on the ground. A comparison between the GPX file and map should see you on the right track.

Scottish Outdoor Access Code and responsible access

The Land Reform (Scotland) Act 2003 grants responsible access across Scotland by bike; the legislation is set out clearly in the SOAC. The key is understanding that *responsible access* is permitted; there is not an inherent right to roam. For gravel riders, this means sticking to tracks and paths that don't conflict with land use or cause nuisance.

The routes included generally try to avoid working areas like farmyards wherever possible; however, there are sections where you need to pass working farms, operational wind farms or

other sites carefully and considerately. Land use changes over time and temporary restrictions could be in place for things like forestry work or lambing, so be prepared to adapt your route if necessary. If you find locked gates on access tracks for no good reason, they can be reported to the local council's access officer.

Developing Mountain Biking in Scotland's *Do the Ride Thing* is well worth reading as a handy guide to responsible off-road riding in Scotland. www.dmbins.com/riders/do-the-ride-thing

The following good, general guide to open access rights is from Mountaineering Scotland www.mountaineering.scot/access/rights-and-responsibilities

- Access rights for non-motorised users extend to moorland, woods and forests, grassland, margins of fields in which crops are growing, paths and tracks, rivers and lochs, the coast and most parks and open spaces.
- Access rights can be exercised at any time of the day or night.
- Notable exceptions include houses and gardens (defined as areas that are 'intensively managed for the domestic enjoyment of the house'), greens of a golf course and structures considered to be 'industrial' (for example some hydroelectric dams). Construction sites and railway lines are also outside access rights.

Countryside code for gravel riders

- Leave gates as you find them (report locked deer gates to the local council's access officer).
- Always slow down around livestock especially around farms (be particularly careful in lambing season; cows with calves should be avoided).
- Stalking runs from 1 July to 15 February; check Heading for the Scottish Hills to see if there is any stalking where you are planning to go as it is best avoided. You are usually okay on tracks and on a Sunday. www.outdooraccess-scotland.scot/practical-guide-all/heading-scottish-hills
- Grouse and pheasant shooting runs from

12 August to 10 December and again is obviously best avoided where possible.

- Respect worksites including quarries, wind farms and temporary forestry operations. In forests it is not only the falling trees, but also logging trucks and especially harvesting machines that require a wide buffer.
- Always avoid construction sites like wind farms or hydro dams with restricted access. Vehicles on industrial-focused gravel tracks will not be expecting you and can drive fast and cut corners, so slow down and ride with caution.

Public transport

Some buses in the Borders take bikes as standard. *www.bordersbuses.co.uk/bike-friendly-buses*

The provision for taking your bike on trains varies across Scotland; reservations are either not available or compulsory, depending on the route. *www.scotrail.co.uk/plan-your-journey/cycling/bikes-trains*

The Highland Explorer trains, which run between Glasgow and Oban, have new dedicated bike carriages with space for 20 bikes. There are plans to run these from Glasgow to Fort William and Mallaig, with hopes to roll these carriages out to the rest of Scotland. At the time of writing, the trains to Inverness are tricky for cyclists as they only have two bike spaces which need to be pre-booked; the guards also tend not to be flexible in most scenarios. However, both train and bus services are constantly improving, so hopefully it will only get easier to take your bike on public transport. *www.scotrail.co.uk/scotrail-highland-explorer*

The weather and seasons

In Scotland you can't escape the weather, but gravel routes are great because they are mostly on all-weather surfaces that can be ridden in most conditions; however, there are exceptions. Some routes in this book have sections prone to getting muddy or river crossings to avoid when it has been particularly wet. While most notable burn or river crossings are included, not every ford will be mentioned in the description.

For longer day rides wait until late May, as this is prime adventure riding season in Scotland, with no midges, long hours of daylight and little need for lights. Winter brings the cold, lack of daylight and frequent snow cover, but gravel tracks hold up well and it shouldn't stop you riding with the right clothing and consideration given to lying snow cover and high water levels.

The best months in Scotland for riding are usually May and June, and September into early October. July and August are often wet, filled with midges and the busiest tourist season too, while winter can be snowy and unpredictable.

Check the weather forecast before your ride, to give you a rough idea of what to expect. The Mountain Weather Information Service is good for the higher routes. *www.mwis.org.uk* *www.metoffice.gov.uk*

Safety and responsibility

It can't be said enough that these gravel routes are all pretty serious excursions into wild and remote parts of Scotland, so plan ahead and be prepared. The routes are not particularly technical, but they deliver you relatively quickly into the hills where experience and basic safety skills are needed. If things go wrong, you can be a long way from help and from any mobile phone reception.

You must be prepared for the clichéd 'four seasons in one day' Scottish weather, so always pack a waterproof jacket and a warm layer. If you're forced to stop it is surprising how cold you can get within minutes. Always make sure someone knows where you are going and when you'll be back; always have a plan in case things go wrong.

Make sure that you carry a well-stocked outdoor first aid kit, even just for cleaning up some gravel rash! On gravel rides ticks are still

Kit list
Safety
- Helmet
- Hi-viz belt/strips for road sections
- First aid kit
- Survival bag
- Whistle
- Fully charged phone in waterproof bag
- GPS device, compass and maps
- Buff (for warmth, but can be used as a makeshift sling)
- Waterproof jacket and spare warm layer
- Emergency sweets or energy gels as well as adequate food and drink

Bike
- Quality multi-tool with chain breaker, Allen keys, spoke key, screwdriver, torx and small blade
- Pump, tube and tyre levers
- Tubeless repair kit (if needed) and patch for tyre rips
- Pliers or tool to remove stuck tubeless valve
- Spare gear hanger (attaches the rear gear mech, if your bike has one)
- Spare chain links
- Spare brake pads, bolts for clipless cleats, chainring bolt and any rack or mount eyelet bolts needed
- Zip ties and spare gaffer tape wrapped around pump
- Charged front and rear lights
- Frame, saddle or bar bag to carry all your kit in

a concern; they can carry Lyme disease and other parasites. A dedicated tick remover is essential for travelling in Scotland. In spring through to autumn, always do a body check after a ride through bracken and vegetation, however lightly it touched you.

Midges tend to be just an annoyance rather than a serious problem; on a gravel bike you can normally leave them behind. Off the bike you'll need Smidge and a head net when bikepacking.

In the event of an accident
If you do get into difficulties and require help, dial **999** or **112** and ask for the **Police** and then **Mountain Rescue**. Make sure you can communicate where you are either using paper map coordinates or using an app on your phone (OS Locate is ideal). If you have intermittent phone signal, an SMS message may send when a call will not connect.

Recommended kit list
Kit taken is subjective and varies between rides, season, and even the time of day. Check the weather forecast when you're planning your ride, but don't take a favourable weather forecast as a reason to leave essential kit out.

The list on the left covers the essentials needed on most rides. The list could go on, but it is important to realise you need a lot more kit than on a road ride, because the consequences are higher in these remote places. Use common sense to add to it depending on time of year and specific route. A frame or bar bag is strongly recommended for gravel riding, so you don't need to carry a backpack.

Bikepacking
Gravel riding and bikepacking go hand in hand perfectly. Bikepacking is a great way to link these routes together or break the longer rides into more manageable weekend overnighters. Bikepacking is simply strapping overnight essentials to your bike and a wee hip flask (ideally filled with Islay whisky). Bikepacking does not always mean camping or a bothy, it could be a remote youth hostel or B&Bs booked ahead to reduce kit needed and enjoy the ride more. There are tips throughout the book on which routes can be linked for longer adventures, or how to use the train to extend a loop into a longer, linear ride.

With ever increasing numbers enjoying the countryside,

OPPOSITE ONE OF WADE'S MILITARY ROAD BRIDGES; SEE ROUTE 19 FOR MORE.

it is more important than ever to act responsibly when wild camping. Essentially: carry out what you take in, do not start fires unless in a designated area and leave no trace.

Bothies are easier than ever to find and as a result many get busy on weekends, but they're still a great option for bikepacking adventures. Most, but not all, are managed by the Mountain Bothies Association, who promote a simple code of conduct to make their use sustainable and fair. Always take a tent or bivvy bag, in case the bothy is full or locked. This book deliberately does not include the location of many bothies, but they can easily be looked up online. *www.mountainbothies.org.uk*

A brief history of gravel in Scotland

This might sound duller than a chat about gravel tyres, but the context of where you ride adds so much to the experience. The gravel tracks we ride have a rich heritage that is at the very heart of Scottish identity. When exploring a new area, it really helps to understand the history of where you are and why this track was built in the first place.

As is so often the case, we start with the Romans and the legendary roads they left behind. While Hadrian's Wall is often seen as the limit of the Roman Empire, the Romans did venture further north; only in the north-west of Scotland did the wrath of the Highlanders finally deter them. The main Roman legacy is in the south of Scotland – some evidence remains of Dere Street (a Roman road running from York to the Edinburgh area) in the tracks and roads around Hawick and the Lammermuirs in the Scottish Borders.

Next up are maybe the most evocative of Scottish tracks: the ancient drove roads. These were used to walk cattle to markets or trysts. Drovers were tough Scots who almost always slept outdoors by their herd with just a wool plaid to wrap around them at night – no fancy merino wool or Gore-Tex® backpacking kit needed. Most routes headed towards Falkirk and Crieff, where the biggest trysts were held. The roads go as far as the Western Isles and Skye and a lot of Scottish cattle were, unbelievably, driven south for weeks to Smithfield Market in London. Drovers sought out routes away from the main roads to save paying tolls and to get good grazing above the busier glens. Many of these routes faded away into the heather but quite a few still exist and are featured in routes here such as **03 Selkirk, Three Brethren and the Bowhill Estate**. In the Cairngorms, these tracks follow natural features like the Gaick Pass (near **20 Dalwhinnie, Loch Ericht and Laggan** and **21 Glen**

Feshie and Loch an Eilein and the Lairig an Laoigh (Gaelic for 'pass of the calves') (north of **16 Linn of Dee, Glen Lui and Linn of Quoich**). Applecross' spectacular road riding climb Bealach na Bà, 'pass of the cattle', is another classic example and, while not included in a route in this book, it is worth cycling if you like a challenge. *The Drove Roads of Scotland* by A.R.B. Haldane covers the history of these roads in more detail.

Several tracks are referred to as 'coffin roads'; these tracks took the most direct line on foot from a settlement to the nearest consecrated ground. You'll see them marked on maps, but few are gravel-bike-friendly, as they take a direct path through rugged and steep hillsides which pushes the abilities of modern mountain bikers.

The herring roads are a well-known feature in the Lammermuirs (see **05 The herring roads of the Lammermuirs**). As you might expect, these tracks are upgraded remnants of the routes that traders used to carry herring caught off the east coast of Scotland to the inland villages in centuries past.

Military history dominates gravel riding with the common description 'Old Military Road' seen on Scottish OS maps. The eighteenth century was when many of today's roads or gravel tracks were created. In 1745–1746, the Jacobite rising led by Charles Edward Stuart (Bonnie Prince Charlie) was roundly defeated by the British government at Culloden, near Inverness. In order to maintain peace and effectively quash uprisings, the government ordered General George Wade to build a series of new roads and forts to control the notoriously inaccessible Highlands. Many of those roads are still in use today as tarmac roads but a significant number are gravel or cobbled. The most famous of the routes is probably the Corrieyairack Pass linking Fort Augustus with the atmospheric ruins of Ruthven Barracks near Aviemore. Wade was also responsible for almost all the remaining old stone arch bridges you'll pass along the way too.

The network was subsequently expanded considerably under the direction of Major William Caulfeild, although his name has now largely been forgotten.

Jumping a century or so forward, after the Highland Clearances had decimated the countryside populations, the new estates of the landed gentry were all about sheep farming, deer stalking and grouse shooting. The hills were now empty, but tracks were built to manage the land and to take deer down off the hills. It was the shift from horseback to four-by-fours that really opened up a steady stream of new access tracks. However, many of these hill tracks are dead ends or very steep, which can be quite frustrating when planning a route. They are also becoming an ugly scar on many of Scotland's upland landscapes with minimal to zero planning permission required to rip up the heather and build these tracks.

The next big impact on the landscape and gravel riding was the Forestry Commission, which was founded in 1919, and with it came mass tree planting on an industrial scale and the ubiquitous 'fire road' or forest track that make up so many of the routes seen in this book. Forest tracks are normally reliable surfaces for gravel bikes, but the challenge is linking them up beyond the forest boundary and into more interesting loops to ride. The original Forestry Commission mountain bike trails of the early twenty-first century were in part built to take bikes off these routes. Things have come full circle as trails got more technical and riders sought out adventures deeper and further through remote forests.

The rise of wind farms has seen the biggest recent impact on the Scottish gravel landscape. These tracks are often at a good climbing gradient and on the tops of hills; however, the challenge is again linking them up into rides because they tend to only access the turbines and not link into other routes.

These modern gravel track developments are almost universally disliked by hillwalkers and mountaineers, but for the gravel rider they provide new access points to leave the cars and roads behind. These tracks are industrial infrastructure – always bear in mind that logging trucks and vehicles will not be expecting cyclists. It is your responsibility to ride safely and always be prepared to get out of the way if needed.

Reading the Gaelic landscape

This glossary of Gaelic place names adds context to Scottish map reading, which opens up a deeper understanding of the places and landscape. Read more on Scottish place names in *Reading the Gaelic Landscape: Leughadh Aghaidh na Tìre*, by John Murray.

abhainn . . . . river
allt . . . . . a burn, or small stream
beag . . . . little
bealach . . . . pass, col
beinn . . . . mountain
buachaille . . . . shepherd
buidhe . . . . yellow
càrn . . . . pile of stones
ceann . . . . head, headland
coille . . . . wood, forest
coire . . . . corrie, hollow in a hill
creag . . . . crag, cliff
damh, daimh . . . . stag
dearg . . . . red
drochaid . . . . bridge
dubh . . . . black
dùn . . . . fortress, castle
eas, easan . . . . waterfall
fèith . . . . bog
fraoch . . . . heather
gleann . . . . . narrow valley, glen
inbhir . . . place of meeting of rivers
làirig . . . . pass
loch . . . . lake, fjord
lochan . . . . small lake
monadh . . . . mountain
mòr . . . . big
rathad . . . . road
ruadh . . . . red, brown
sgòrr, sgùrr . . . sharp, rocky peak
strath . . . . . . wide river valley
taigh . . . . house
uaine . . . . green
uisge . . . . water

RIDGETOP RIDING NEAR THE THREE BRETHREN (ROUTE 03).

SCOTTISH
BORDERS

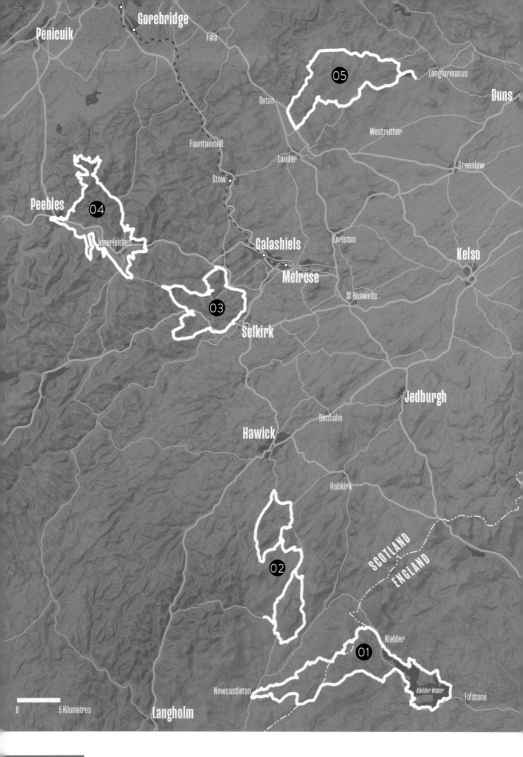

SCOTTISH BORDERS

The first selection of routes is mostly in the Scottish Borders – one route crosses the border into England and another traverses a section of the border with neighbouring East Lothian. This large, sparsely inhabited region offers some of the wildest and least explored places in the UK, and with this comes a feeling of genuine isolation and pioneering adventure along these routes. The Southern Uplands are rolling, but deceptively big, hills; they are blanketed in heather but punctuated by large plantation forests and pockets of native woodland too. This all rolls down to the mighty lowland rivers fabled for trout and salmon fishing but which also powered the first hydro textile mills of Scotland.

The Tweed Valley in the Borders is probably the best place in the UK for mountain biking. However, few will know this area for its out-standing, quiet road riding and of course the endless unexplored gravel routes on ancient drove roads, forest roads, new wind farm access tracks and farm tracks. There are also fewer midges than most parts of Scotland, making summer here even more attractive.

Broad Law is the highest peak in the region; at 840 metres it is below Munro height, which helps to preserve its solitude as it does not attract Munro baggers. There is also a gravel track that rises to the summit – it's a brutal, relentless climb up to the summit's radar station which, on a misty day, leaves you wondering whether a UFO has landed.

Castles and large stately homes, such as Sir Walter Scott's Abottsford or historic Traquair House, dot the landscape. It is a playground for adventure and getting away from it all.

01 NEWCASTLETON TO KIELDER CROSS-BORDER RIDE

72KM/45 MILES

Introduction

This gravel ride uses the very best tracks in this gravel riding Mecca. Starting in the lovely little village of Newcastleton, the route also offers options to ride some easy mountain bike trails to spice things up. The evocatively named Bloody Bush MTB Trail over the moors is a techy gravel highlight.

The local area

This cross-border gravel route feels a good place to start the book. Although this route starts in Scotland, it crosses the English border early on and actually covers more ground in England. In the area around Kielder it is hard to choose a route because there are just so many gravel tracks; it's home to the Dirty Reiver (a famous 200-kilometre gravel riding event) for a reason!

The village of Newcastleton is a great place to start; this Victorian planned village is also known as Copshaw Holm and, just to confuse you, different maps do use the different names! It was founded in 1793 by the Duke of Buccleuch, whose estate still owns most of the south of Scotland as you'll read in the nearby route descriptions. Here, members of a community trust have raised funds and buy 750 acres of land to manage themselves. It might hardly make a dent in the 200,000 acres the Duke's estate owns, but it presents a huge opportunity for the community to take a fresh approach to land management.

The route uses the waymarked Cross Border Trail; this border region has previously been a lot less peaceful than you'll find it today – from the Romans in the first century,

OPPOSITE CROSSING THE BORDER INTO ENGLAND VIA A SLIPPERY BRIDGE.

DISTANCE **72km/45 miles** — ASCENT **950m/3,117ft** — OFF-ROAD **over 90%**
START/FINISH **Newcastleton (also known as Copshaw Holm)**
START/FINISH GRID REF **NY 483875** — SATNAV **TD9 0QD**
GPS **55.1791, -2.8134** — MAP OS **Landranger 79, Hawick & Eskdale;
80, Cheviot Hills & Kielder Water (1:50,000)**

GRAVEL SCALE

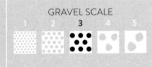

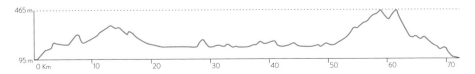

A TECHY SECTION ALONG THE RED BLOODY BUSH MTB TRAIL.

Navigation

This route crosses some very remote and isolated forests and fells between Newcastleton and Kielder. Even the village centre of Kielder has no phone reception. However, most of it is waymarked, making navigation easier and helping out in what can be a confusing forest.

The route must be ridden anticlockwise as it uses some official mountain bike trails that must be ridden in this direction. Initially you follow the Cross Border Trail with its flags and purple waymarkers, then the Sustrans National Route 10 blue markers around Kielder Water, and finally it uses an optional section of the red Bloody Bush MTB Trail. The Cross Border Trail is not well used, and posts can be hidden when grass grows around the posts. There is one

through early Christian battles, to the invasion of the Normans after 1066 and the long conflicts between the English and the Scots. This ride is at the heart of what was the frontier zone and the Debatable Lands, where raids and counter raids took place for centuries with clashes across the wild moors. The legacy of the Border Reivers can be seen in the ruined towers, castles and ancient monuments.

The Bloody Bush MTB Trail goes past the site of the defeat and death of a party of Northumbrians returning from a foray into Liddesdale in the fifteenth century; they were resting in a thicket when slain. The monument you see today stands exactly on the border and is over 4 metres high.

The loop around Kielder Water is a brilliant section of the ride. Kielder Water is at the heart of a huge forest and is the largest man-made lake in Northern Europe; the multi-use path around the reservoir includes a crossing of Kielder Viaduct, a rare skewed-arch viaduct. The area is also an official Dark Sky Park, so it is worth staying overnight too.

Route overview

The route mostly uses good quality commercial forest tracks and the well-surfaced Lakeside Way around Kielder Water. The route is pretty wild and committing – it doesn't have many sections on roads and there isn't a lot of mobile phone coverage. When you're away from the reservoir you'll most likely see no other people, so go prepared for a big day with potentially unpredictable weather.

The route is rated 3 for gravel mostly because of two sections

1 THE CLIMB BACK INTO SCOTLAND PAST THE BLOODY BUSH MONUMENT. **2** THE REMARKABLE SKEWED ARCHES OF KIELDER VIADUCT.

of rougher singletrack around Bloody Bush. A few sections of the Cross Border Trail along Kershope Burn are on quite coarse gravel and include some singletrack too.

A real highlight is the rollercoaster-like Kielder Water Lakeside Way path, which is smooth and fast, but it can be busy with walkers around Kielder village and the dam to the south. For this reason, the route detours on to forest road sections to avoid the busiest parts.

The return leg from Kielder to Newcastleton has a section of red mountain bike trail. It is rideable but very bumpy with large cobbles on the initial climb; the descent is smoother and lots of fun, although it is getting a bit overgrown. You can opt to stay on the track and detour around to the Bloody Bush monument climb. This climb is a very narrow gravel singletrack (nature has started to reclaim the trail); it isn't too technical but takes some concentration. This section is also very exposed to the wind and rain (or sunshine).

After the Bloody Bush MTB Trail the gravel track descent is fast, but look carefully for a left-hand turn as the Cross Border Trail waymarker is almost hidden by vegetation. After the waymarker, the next section is around 100 metres of eroded singletrack.

The ride finishes with options for gravel-bike-friendly descents on the blue (or red) mountain bike trails at Newcastleton, which is one of the 7stanes mountain bike trail centres which range across the south of Scotland. Once on the trails they are waymarked back to the start.

post in particular that is on the fast, penultimate descent after the Bloody Bush section that can be easily missed. If you do miss it, you'll miss some good riding and end up on the road back to Newcastleton.

Facilities and refreshments
Newcastleton is a great place to start with a range of shops, cafes and plenty of parking in the village centre. **The Olive Tree** is a great place for coffee while **Copshaw Kitchen** serves up standard, hearty cafe food. There are no other facilities along the route except at Kielder Water. There are cafes around the reservoir itself, but the best option is **Kielder Castle Cafe** (just off-route at Kielder village), it also has Wi-Fi which might be useful due to the lack of phone reception.

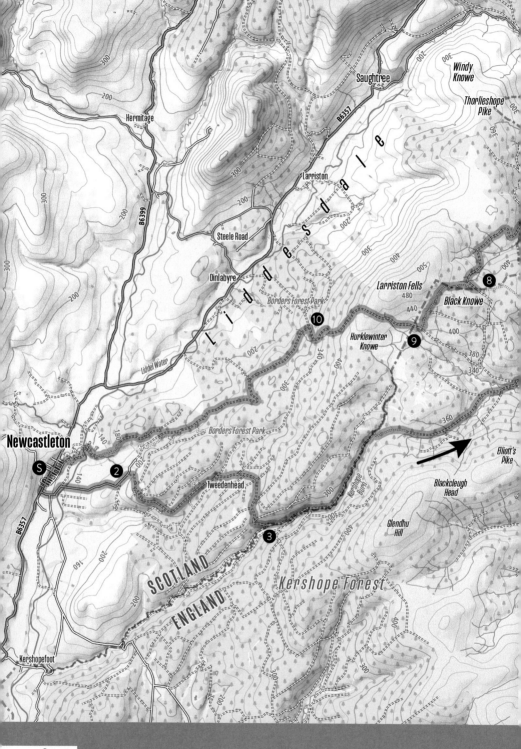

Deadwater
Deadwater Fell
Wether Lair
Monkside
Greys Pike
Kielder
❼
❻
Kielder Forest
Bakethin Reservoir
White Knowe
Well Holes
Lewis Burn
❹
Rushy Knowe
Menshaw Burn
Cock Stoor
Kielder Water
Falstone
Kielder Forest
Bull Crag Peninsula
❺
Merlin Brae
Elf Kirk
Low Cranecleugh

N

0   2 Kilometres

THE STARTING SIGNPOST ON THE CROSS BORDER TRAIL.

Bike shops

The nearest bike shop is some distance away in Hawick, appropriately called **Hawick Cycles** (T: 01450 372 631), with some spares and most repairs.

Public transport and access

There are no practical public transport options. Newcastleton has a campsite, shops and cafes and parking available. Kielder village also has a campsite and there are lakeside cabins at Kielder Water that make a nice overnight stop.

The route

S From the centre of Newcastleton village head south before turning left over Liddel Water. Carry on along the tarmac until the first purple Cross Border Trail marker points up a gravel track.

2 Follow the gravel track. After 500m the Cross Border Trail turns off right; ignore this overgrown singletrack and keep on the main gravel track.

3 You rejoin the Cross Border Trail markers after a fast descent. A steady climb follows Kershope Burn, which is also the border line. Finally, a wooden bridge takes you over the burn and into England on a narrow gravel path. Keep following the Cross Border Trail and Sustrans National Route 10 until you reach Kielder Water.

4 When you reach the reservoir, to the left is an impressive modern arching pedestrian bridge that goes to Kielder village; keep right to follow the route around the reservoir. The full loop initially uses the waymarked Lakeside Way path, with Sustrans National Route 10 also signposted until you reach the dam at the southern end of the reservoir.

5 Cross the dam. After the dam either stay on our route by following a forest track (called North Haul Road on OS maps), which moves away from the reservoir for a time, or follow the Lakeside Way path (which can be busy). Halfway along the reservoir turn left to leave the North Haul Road to join the Lakeside Way, which is now much quieter.

RIDING ON TOP OF KIELDER VIADUCT.

6 At the end of the lake the trail heads over Kielder Viaduct. This stunning skewed-arch viaduct takes you into Kielder village itself. From Kielder village follow the main road north for less than 1km before reaching an obvious gravel track just before a church building.

7 Turn left on to the track – it heads up and up with wide open views. The navigation isn't waymarked for this section, but it is pretty straightforward to follow the main track.

8 Look out for signposts for the Bloody Bush MTB Trail. Nature is trying its best to reclaim this remote trail and the cobbled rocks will vibrate your fillings out; you can detour around on a track but the MTB trail adds some fun smooth berms down to the Bloody Bush monument.

9 The singletrack climb after the monument is very narrow, down to almost a tyre width in places, but it is gravel under-tyre and a good challenge. The climbing is almost over when you see a phone mast appear ahead. On the fast gravel descent that follows, keep your eyes peeled – you don't want to miss the Cross Border Trail waymarker post pointing to the left.

10 After this turn off on to singletrack, there is 100m of trail which is badly eroded and has a nasty, steep stream crossing, before it joins a perfect gravel track. Follow the Cross Border Trail signs back to Newcastleton. There are options to take red or blue trails back down; they all end at the same place.

Other routes or attractions in the area

The route does have an option to shorten it – head north, rather than south, when you reach Kielder Water to avoid a full lap of the reservoir.

The potential for quality gravel riding is endless in this area, but looking at the Dirty Reiver event and route is a good start. The gravel is usually smooth here on the plantation forest tracks and in the rolling foothills of the Scottish Borders and Cheviots. This route is designed to link into **02 Hawick castles and railways loop** (pages 13–19).

02 HAWICK CASTLES AND RAILWAYS LOOP
60KM/37 MILES

Introduction

This figure-of-eight ride to the south of Hawick takes in some fascinating local history including an abandoned railway and the imposing Hermitage Castle. It uses quality, well-maintained gravel tracks through forests and farmland all linked together by a very pleasant B road as the spine of the route. With over 900 metres of climbing don't underestimate this ride, but there are straightforward options to cut it short.

The local area

The historic textile and market town of Hawick is filled with Borders culture. It is off the tourist trail, but stacked with history and intrigue. The area has a vast untapped seam of gravel riding in the surrounding hills. In fact, the locals have recently launched a website to promote the countryside on Hawick's doorstep. *www.townof1000trails.co.uk*

The route starts and finishes near Stobs Camp and Stobs Castle, a stately home which has a remarkable history which could fill a book by itself. It was purchased in 1903 by the War Office and housed army training camps and then prisoners of war during World War I; it was also used during World War II. The old prisoner of war and military camp is still visible just off the route. It is certainly a creepy place on a dark, misty day; it's worth a quick detour. If it captures your imagination there's plenty of information at *www.stobscamp.org*

The area is home to some notable viaducts and station ruins from the Waverley Route railway, which ran from Edinburgh to

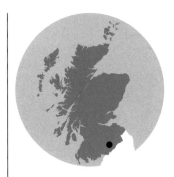

OPPOSITE CLASSIC BORDERS PLANTATION FOREST LANDSCAPE.

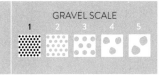

DISTANCE **60km/37 miles** — ASCENT **915m/3,002ft** — OFF-ROAD **50%**
START/FINISH **South of Hawick, near Woodfoot Bridge**
START/FINISH GRID REF **NT 506100** — SATNAV **TD9 9SG**
GPS **55.3815, -2.7812** — MAP **OS Landranger 79, Hawick & Eskdale** **(1:50,000)**

GRAVEL SCALE
1   2   3   4   5

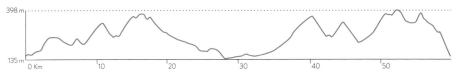

GRAVEL RIDES SCOTLAND

Carlisle and closed in 1969. Part of the line, from Edinburgh to Tweedbank, was reopened with great success in 2015 and there is work ongoing to try and reopen more. This gravel route heads past the remote Riccarton Junction where a branch line bound for Hexham used to split off to the east; it now is an eerie ruin in the middle of a remote forest. It's hard to imagine steam trains passing through on the route to Carlisle then on to London in the 1950s. Later in the ride is Whitrope summit and tunnel, now home to a railway heritage centre that hosts an eclectic collection of trains and carriages in various states of oxidation after losing the battle to the Scottish elements. There is occasionally a cafe in the summer here, but don't rely on it being open.

The other big feature of this route is the powerful and imposing Hermitage Castle; like most strong houses and castles in the Borders it has an association with the Border Reivers. The Border Reivers were a ruthless bunch and 'reivering' was seen as a way of surviving, with loyalties and feuding between families just an accepted way of life. While it was a tough and pretty brutal period of history, Hawick still hosts an annual festival each spring to celebrate and re-enact the Border Reivers!

Route overview

Not only is the route loaded with its own history lesson, the gravel and road riding are genuinely top drawer – there are just so many tracks with sweeping vistas and you'll most likely not meet another soul.

This ride is a figure of eight and therefore offers two clear loops for those put off by the distance or climbing. The short out-and-back road detour to Hermitage Castle is recommended. The full loop is roughly half on the road; the gravel surfaces are all smooth. The only sections to watch out for are after Shankend Viaduct and the final descent, which are on farm tracks and can be a bit muddy and bumpy at times. The track down to Woodfoot Bridge near Stobs is the ride highlight due to the epic views; this section is therefore best ridden in a northerly, or clockwise, direction. The B6399 is understandably a favourite road route for the nearby Hawick Cycling Club, but some corners can be a bit blind for car drivers, so be aware.

Navigation
The route is ridden clockwise to end on the great farm track descent down to the start near Stobs Camp. Navigation is relatively straightforward because you never venture far from the same B road but you do quickly get deep into large and disorientating plantation forests, so be well prepared and note that the mobile signal is very poor throughout.

Facilities and refreshments
Hawick is the closest option for food – it has a full range of shops, cafes and even a world-class Velosolutions Pump Track for an impromptu drop bar skills session if you are brave enough.

Along the actual route there are no facilities other than the occasional cafe at the heritage centre at Whitrope summit. Hermitage Castle has toilets but nothing else; there is an entry fee to visit the castle but it is worth stopping to explore.

OPPOSITE THE IMPRESSIVE SHANKEND VIADUCT.

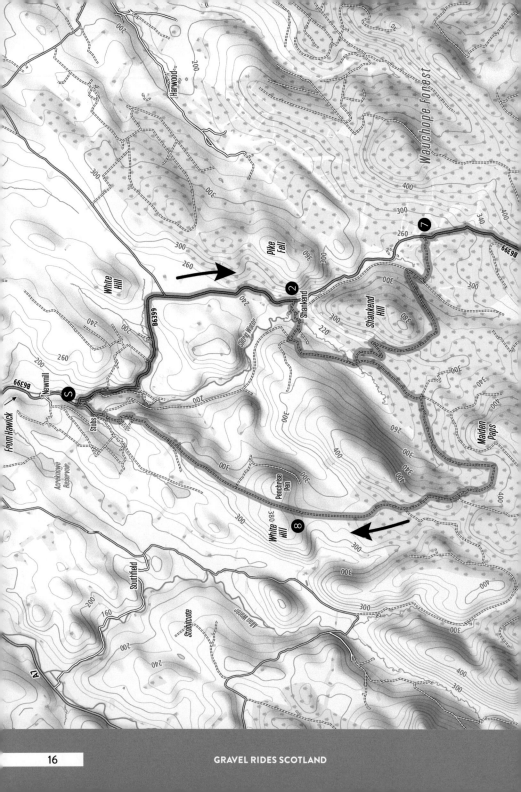

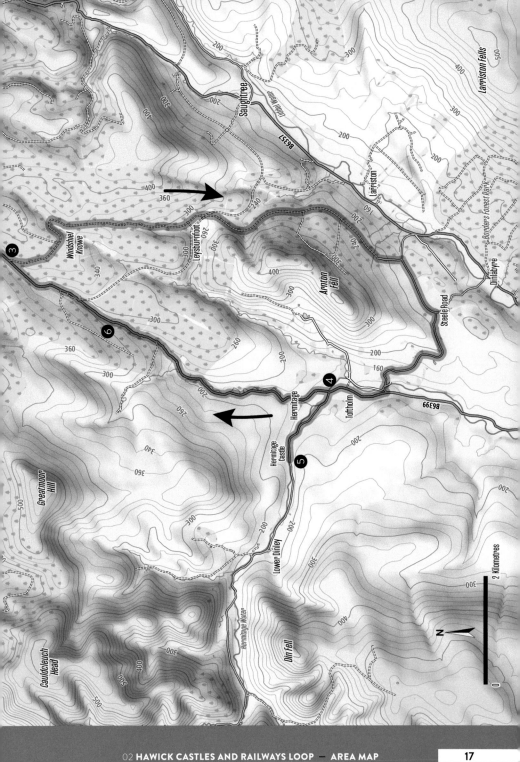

1 HEADING TOWARDS MAIDEN PAPS. **2** LEAVING THE SHANKEND VIADUCT BEHIND.

Bike shops
The nearest bike shop is in Hawick, appropriately called **Hawick Cycles** (T: 01450 372 631), with some spares and most repairs. The recently opened pump track has really spurred cycling in the town.

Public transport and access
The route starts just south of Hawick near Woodfoot Bridge, where there is some limited lay-by parking but no facilities or formal car parking. You could start from one of a number of lay-bys along the B6399 north or here, or add a few more miles and start from Hawick itself.

Unfortunately, useful public transport, as the abandoned railway theme suggests, is now non-existent. The nearest train station is at Tweedbank. The Borders Buses from Edinburgh to Tweedbank do also take bikes internally for free; however they don't carry on any further south yet.

The route

S Near Woodfoot Bridge is a parking lay-by; this area is a natural start point. From here, head south along the B6399 towards Stobs Castle; this is a pleasant warm-up. Carry on until you see the impressive viaduct at Shankend.

2 Turn right at the viaduct and follow the gravel track heading south under the arches. This pleasant farm track climbs then descends into the forest. A left-hand turn takes you on to a forest track, which goes up and down a small hill before briefly joining the old railway line, which can be muddy. Rejoin the B6399 and turn right.

3 Take the next gravel track on the left which heads east through the forest to the abandoned Riccarton Junction. Once you've taken in the surreal setting, it's on to quiet lanes around the southern loop before reaching the B6399 again. Turn right, heading north.

4 After around 1km you reach a junction with the road leading to Hermitage Castle. Hermitage Castle (entry fee) is a short detour from the B6399 (turn left and ride for 1km) – it's worth visiting for a wander around. The castle itself is a Historic Environment Scotland site; check opening times before you visit.

THE IMPOSING BUT BLEAK HERMITAGE CASTLE.

5 From Hermitage Castle return to the B6399 and turn left (heading north) to reach Whitrope summit.

6 At Whitrope summit there is a small heritage centre with railway memorabilia and decaying trains. (Don't be tempted to take the path marked on some maps from Whitrope into the forest; it is technically a shortcut but it's not in great condition. Likewise, the old railway line itself is overgrown and rough in places despite being marked as a track on some maps.)

7 This is the middle section of the figure of eight; continue heading north on the B6399 then turn left on to the same gravel track you used earlier. Continue on perfect gravel riding, turning left before you reach Langside Burn to start the second loop, following the forest track around the volcanic looking conical peak of Maiden Paps.

8 You now leave the forest behind and move on to a long, open descent on a farm track with far reaching views to Hawick and the surrounding hills. Being out in the open and on farmland, it is rough in places but never gets too bad. It is a great finale to a fascinating gravel ride in a less pedalled corner of the country.

Other routes or attractions in the area

You can continue on gravel tracks and the B6399 to Newcastleton, with its mountain bike loops and **01 Newcastleton to Kielder cross-border ride** (pages 5–11), for a longer bikepacking adventure or a bothy overnighter. To the east are back roads and tracks to explore towards Bonchester Bridge, offering easy options to extend this ride in different directions.

03 SELKIRK, THREE BRETHREN AND THE BOWHILL ESTATE
39KM/24 MILES

Introduction

This varied and at times challenging route delivers some classic riding, the highlight being some awesome easy singletrack along a broad ridgetop; this forms part of the Southern Upland Way and offers expansive views across moorland and forests. An epic descent on a drove road delivers you to the romantically named Duchess's Drive, offering some rather stately gravel riding to end on.

The local area

Selkirk is a traditional Borders town built on textile mills harnessing the power of the Ettrick Water. There are lots of great routes around the town, whether road, MTB or gravel. While the moors are dramatic, lower down the landscape turns to luscious deciduous woodland, especially on the Bowhill Estate; in between are the familiar plantation forest and fields of sheep.

Like many towns in the Borders, Selkirk celebrates an annual common ridings festival, an event where locals ride horses around the boundary of the town's land, which includes the Three Brethren cairns passed on our route. The Selkirk Common Riding is the largest cavalcade of horses in the Borders' common riding season with over 400 riders on horseback taking part. If you happen to be visiting in June (when the weather is often best too), it is worth trying to catch this or another of the Borders' common riding festivals.

The Three Brethren is an iconic landmark located at one of the highest points on the route. As you approach you will clearly see the three large cairns, each over 2 metres tall and

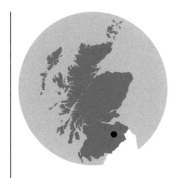

OPPOSITE THE INTRIGUING AND SCENIC SETTING OF THE THREE BRETHREN.

DISTANCE **39km/24 miles** ▬ ASCENT **880m/2,887ft** ▬ OFF-ROAD **65%**
START/FINISH **Western edge of Selkirk, near Selkirk Rugby Football Club**
START/FINISH GRID REF **NT 459286** ▬ SATNAV **TD7 5AZ**
GPS **55.5481, -2.8590** ▬ MAP **OS Landranger 73, Peebles, Galashiels & Selkirk (1:50,000)**

GRAVEL SCALE

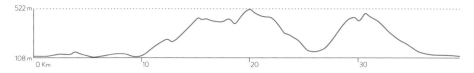

GRAVEL RIDES SCOTLAND

marking the meeting of the boundaries of Selkirk Burgh, Yair and Buccleuch, three historic estates. The loop also takes in the elegant Duchess's Drive within the Bowhill Estate; this track was a Victorian carriage drive and is now a classic gravel route over moorland tops and through wonderful deciduous forests – look out for the Duke's stone seat on the way down. Bowhill House itself belongs to the Duke of Buccleuch who owns most of southern Scotland; this vast house is one of his holiday homes. Buccleuch's Borders Estate covers an obscene 127,000 acres. The Duke's other holiday homes include Drumlanrig Castle, part of the comparably pokey 83,000-acre Queensberry Estate, and he probably has a fancy static caravan parked up somewhere near the coast too. The gardens at Bowhill, and occasionally part of the house, are open to the public and it's a nice place to explore, especially with kids.

Route overview

At 'just' 39 kilometres don't let this route deceive you; it has plenty of punch and rewards with over 800 metres of climbing. August is a great time to visit as the heather is in full bloom and the hills turn into a rich sea of purple for just a brief window.

This route utilises two main singletrack sections on the infamous drove road network in the Borders. The first of these sections from the Three Brethren varies between smooth dirt, pockets of mud and stony paths. The section down to the Yarrow Valley is narrow singletrack with a few bumps to watch for; it can be a bit overgrown in late summer, which hides some of the bumps, so keep alert. Some riders may prefer a mountain bike or suspension for these two sections, but it is certainly well within the realms of gravel riding. Just avoid it when it has been too wet or if you run slick tyres.

Duchess's Drive is a lot of fun and is all on good quality Victorian gravel; however, when riding close to Bowhill House remember it is a popular area so slow down and watch out for walkers and horse riders on the final descent. Note that an entry fee is charged for Bowhill House, the gardens and a great kids play park (they are exempt from SOAC). Access to the wider estate that this route uses is free and responsible users are welcomed under SOAC and by the estate, but just be aware of this restriction.

Navigation

The best direction to ride this route is anticlockwise, the logic being that the big singletrack descent is best done this way and it gets the busiest road section out the way when you're fresh at the start. Once you're on the loop you're pretty much committed, with no real shortcut options. It is relatively challenging to navigate through Yair Hill Forest near the start but the Southern Upland Way is waymarked and the Duchess's Drive track is relatively clear to follow.

Facilities and refreshments

Be warned: Selkirk town centre with its many shops, takeaways and cafes is up a rather large hill, so save a bit of energy if needed. The **Waterwheel Tea Room** is a popular stop for road cyclists and is perfectly located near the end on the road from Bowhill back to Selkirk. There is also a cafe at Bowhill House but technically it is within the house grounds which have an entry fee to access, so ask first.

1 SIGNPOST FOR THE OLD DROVE ROAD TO YARROW.

2 SUMMIT OF BROWN KNOWE.

3 WINTERY FOREST RIDING IN YAIR.

4 SUNSET BEFORE THE DESCENT TO THE YARROW VALLEY.

5 GOLDEN HOUR AT THE BROWN KNOWE CAIRN.

SUMMER EVENING PERFECTION ON THE SOUTHERN UPLAND WAY.

Bike shops

Scott's Cycle Services (T: 07432 408 928) is a relatively new bike shop in Selkirk, with spares and repairs.

Public transport and access

Parking is easiest in Selkirk and the route starts at a parking area near the rugby club.

Selkirk is off the railway network; the nearest station is at nearby Tweedbank, where the Borders Buses (which carry bikes for free) also stop. The Borders Buses, which have four spaces internally for bikes, mean you can easily link to **04 Four forests and a wind farm in the Tweed Valley** (pages 29–35) without a car and then get back to Edinburgh. You can't book a space for your bike, but getting a space usually isn't a problem; the Borders Buses app has more details.

The route

🅂 The route starts from Selkirk on what is the only real section of road; it can be a bit busy so ride aware.

❷ After about 6km you reach traffic lights at the impressive and historic Yair Bridge, spanning over some rare rapids in the River Tweed; it's also a popular fishing spot. Instead of following the road at the traffic lights keep heading straight ahead on to the gravel track. The track is generally flat but gets bumpy in places. It follows near the mighty River Tweed; watch for machinery and animals as you ride past a farmyard.

❸ Before the track joins a tarmac back road, make sure you take a left turn. Be warned – this climb goes on and on. Some careful navigation is needed in Yair Hill Forest, which is a generic plantation forest. It can be disorienting, but you basically need to head up and up on the main track until you reach a high point. The final push to the top is a steep challenge but it can be ridden without dabbing on a gravel bike – gauntlet thrown down!

❹ You now reach a saddle on the Southern Upland Way. Looking left you'll see what appears to be a near-vertical track up to the Three Brethren cairns – it isn't as bad as it looks! The views, especially over to the conical Eildon Hills to the east, make a quick detour up to the cairns worthwhile. Once a snack has

1 THE THREE BRETHREN UP CLOSE. **2** PLANTATION FOREST RIDING IN YAIR.

been eaten and legs rested, start descending back down the Southern Upland Way, heading west. This next ridgetop section is a classic mountain bike route, and it is a lot of fun on a gravel bike.

5 After about 6km on the undulating ridgetop, turn left (signposted *Cross Borders Drove Road towards the Yarrow Valley*) and descend some sweet, narrow and bumpy but drop-bar-friendly singletrack. It's pushing the technical level so keep concentrating all the way to the first gate.

6 To get down to Yarrow Water there are some steps to negotiate before reaching the road. Turn left along the road then, after the bridge over the Yarrow Water, turn right on to a minor road then turn right again on to Duchess's Drive on the Bowhill Estate, which is all classic gravel. Just beware of navigating a few left turns heading up to the high point. The forest is temporarily left behind to reveal views in all directions.

7 The descent is fast and fun but watch out for other users as you head towards the house; it is tempting to absolutely let rip along this track, but horses often use it so hold back a bit. Stop for a cake and coffee in the Waterwheel Tea Room on the road back to Selkirk before cruising back to your starting point. Your legs will feel like they've done more than 39km, that's for sure!

Other routes or attractions in the area
This route can be extended in many ways; most options are to the south and west, including heading over towards Peebles and joining **04 Four forests and a wind farm in the Tweed Valley** (pages 29–35). There are just too many tracks and options – for bikepacking carry on north-east and you can join sections of the Capital Trail finishing in Edinburgh. The Capital Trail was designed as a mountain bike route, but the parts through the Lammermuirs are all track-based.

04 FOUR FORESTS AND A WIND FARM IN THE TWEED VALLEY
66KM/41 MILES

Introduction

This route, if ridden in full, is an epic. It starts by climbing through the mountain bike Mecca of Glentress Forest before taking you on some sublime gravel up to Bowbeat Wind Farm, which has epic views as far Edinburgh and the Firth of Forth. The short but very steep turbine 13 climb is a locals' challenge; it is luckily followed by a fast, never-ending descent before continuing for three extra loops in three different forests.

The local area

The Tweed Valley is known for being the best mountain bike destination in the UK, but there is just so much more to explore. From Moffat to Innerleithen, there are countless gravel loops in the hills, forests and increasingly in the new wind farms. The gigantic Clyde Wind Farm near Moffat can provide many days' worth of gravel tracks.

This route starts in the Royal Burgh of Peebles, a great little town that has retained one of the most independent high streets in Scotland. The area really understands cycling – the Tweed Valley Railway Path is an off-road cycle path through the valley from Walkerburn to Peebles and there are plenty of bike-friendly places to stay, such as the Peebles Hydro or Tontine hotels through to camping pods at Glentress.

Bowbeat Wind Farm is the high point of the ride; with 24 identical turbines it can be a bit confusing to navigate, but you can see Edinburgh Castle and Arthur's Seat on a clear day. The site is so high and remote that it took a lot of new tracks and one

OPPOSITE LOOKING BACK DOWN TO PEEBLES FROM GLENTRESS.

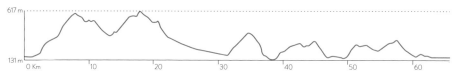

DISTANCE **66km/41 miles** — ASCENT **1,524m/5,000ft** — OFF-ROAD **80%**
START/FINISH **Peebles** — START/FINISH GRID REF **NT 250403**
SATNAV **EH45 8AW** — GPS **55.6504, -3.1934** — MAP **OS Landranger 73, Peebles, Galashiels & Selkirk (1:50,000)**

GRAVEL SCALE
1 2 3 4 5

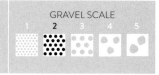

617 m

131 m

0 Km   10   20   30   40   50   60

GRAVEL RIDES SCOTLAND

year to build, but it also has one of the highest average wind speeds of any UK land wind farm so it produces a lot of power.

Leithen Lodge is about halfway through the route and is an eye-catching orange and green historic lodge; it is an example of Arts and Crafts architecture and a wonderfully wacky building in the middle of nowhere. It has self-catering apartments and is quite popular with mountain bikers who are riding in the area and looking for a bit of luxury.

Finally, the route passes Traquair House, the oldest inhabited house in Scotland and home to the Stuart family since 1491. You ride past the Bear Gates, locked in 1745 following the visit of Bonnie Prince Charlie when the fifth Earl of Traquair promised they would never be opened again, until the Stuarts returned to the throne. It also has a brewery that makes tasty, but pretty strong, beer.

Route overview

The route has a gravel rating of 2; while it is all on good surfaces a few tracks do get into quite chunky gravel and there is one short section heading out of Elibank and Traquair Forest that gets wet and a bit muddy. This section is part of the Southern Upland Way and, along with the descent from the wind farm, is the reason for riding in a clockwise direction as they make fun descents.

The initial climb of the route through Glentress Forest offers the chance to add in some of the blue mountain bike trails which are drop-bar-friendly. The red and black routes are generally too rough and really need suspension to enjoy.

The descents out of Glentress and from Bowbeat Wind Farm are flat-out fast but you will find weak tyres out as you clatter through a few short sections of quite angular gravel at speed. As with all wind farms, watch out in winter for falling ice from the blades as you ride underneath.

There is undeniably a lot of up and down in this route and over 1,500 metres of climbing can feel daunting; however, if your legs fail you there are many options to cut it short. Once past the golf course north of Innerleithen you can divert to a cafe, then follow the Tweed Valley Railway Path along the River Tweed back to Peebles with no more hills. Before each of the remaining forest sections you can either cut on to this cycle path or take the B7062 back to Peebles – all but the bravest will probably opt to do this!

Navigation
The route is best ridden clockwise due to the descents and climbs being best in this direction. Navigation can be hard work in all the plantation forests and on the wind farm in particular; both can be disorientating even in fine weather so be ready to take out your map and compass or use a reliable GPS device. The wind farm has regular site maps to help, but they aren't the easiest to read.

Facilities and refreshments
The route is very well served for cafes and good food with plenty of options throughout. In Peebles look for **Coltman's Kitchen, Deli & Bar** and **Coco Black** for patisserie quality cakes and world class chocolates. Other places to visit would be **Forsyths of Peebles** for a quality lasagne pie (yes pasta and pastry), **No1 Peebles Road** in Innerleithen and **Caberston Coffee Shop** in Walkerburn. **Nashy's** is just off the Tweed Valley Railway Path in Cardrona village in the old train station. Cardrona also has a well-designed little pump track too.

OPPOSITE THE CHALLENGING CLIMB TOWARDS BOWBEAT WIND FARM.

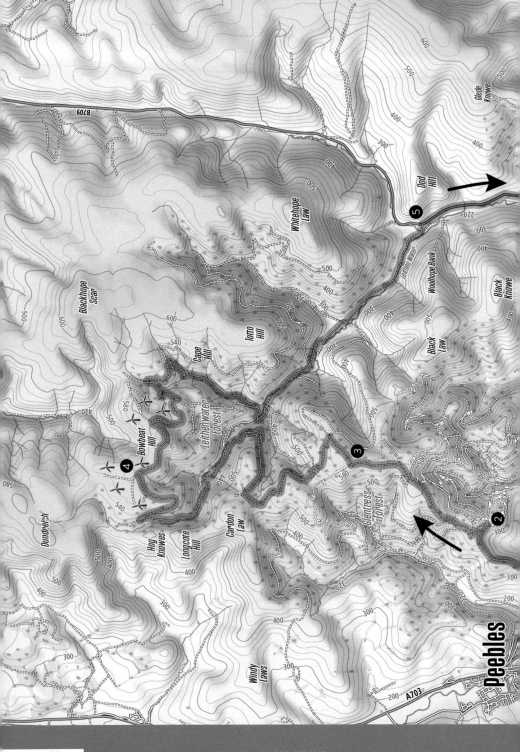

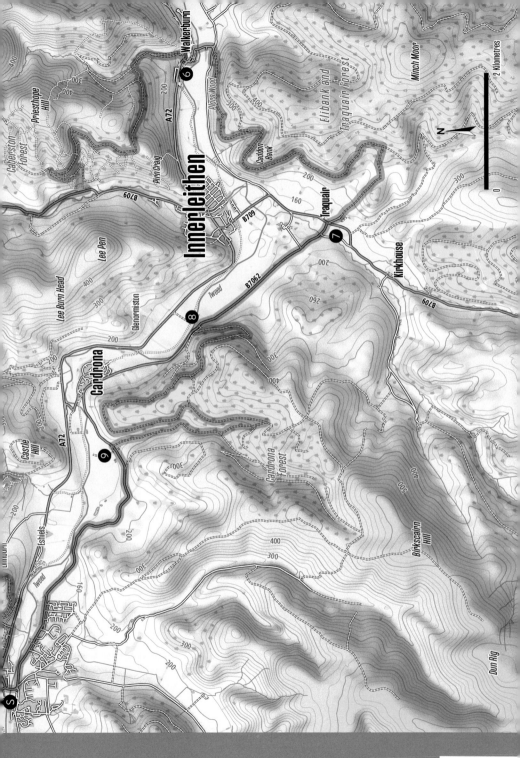

MOORLAND RIDING IN THE TWEED VALLEY.

Bike shops

Being a huge mountain biking centre, there are loads of bike shops between Peebles and Innerliethen so you'll hopefully get sorted for just about anything, if they can fit you in. The best options are **Alpine Bikes** (T: 01721 724 522) at Glentress, **Tweed Valley Bikes** (T: 01896 831 429) in Innerleithen and Peebles, **i-cycles** (T: 01896 829 680) Innerleithen and **BSpoke** (T: 01721 723 423) in Peebles.

Public transport and access

There is ample free parking in Peebles; it might be tempting to park at Glentress Forest, but parking isn't free and the cafe option is not as good for a post-ride stop.

While Peebles has not been on a train line since the 1950s, the Borders Buses (which carry bikes for free) run from Edinburgh to Tweedbank via Peebles.

The route

S From the centre of Peebles join the Tweed Valley Railway Path beyond the Peebles Hydro Hotel; soon after joining this tarmac path turn left on to a gravel track up through Janet's Brae beech woodland, part of Glentress Forest.

2 At the top you reach the Buzzard's Nest car park, where there is a freeride bike area and some blue and green trails. This area has planning permission to build a large number of holiday cabins; bear this in mind in case it looks very different when you visit. Before an obvious stone quarry, turn left then first right on to Anderson Road – it is relentlessly uphill. Make sure that you stop to catch your breath and look back to admire the outstanding view behind you.

3 Just before you reach Dunslair Heights (which is just over 600m and has a tall aerial), turn right on to a bit of techy doubletrack with grass down the middle. You have now left Glentress Forest – it gets quieter and navigating becomes more of a challenge so keep that map handy.

4 Keep heading on to reach Bowbeat Knowe and Bowbeat Hill. The latter reaches a height of 626m, is brutally steep and hosts the infamous turbine 13; on a windy day it sounds like the blades above will take your head off. The descent takes in a couple of switchbacks – steep and fast. The run out at the bottom gets fast but is rougher so watch your speed.

RESTING ON THE STEEP TURBINE 13 CLIMB.

5 Turn right on to the B709 then turn left into Caberston Forest, where a simple gravel track with open views over Innerleithen drops you down into Walkerburn. The route goes right past the popular Caberston Coffee Shop in Walkerburn.

6 From Walkerburn, head into the Elibank and Traquair Forest on the opposite side of the River Tweed. (Alternatively, follow the Tweed Valley Railway Path along the Tweed straight back to Peebles.) The first section of track through the forest is used by Adrenalin Uplift minibuses (they mostly run from Fridays to Mondays, but do sometimes run at other times too), so ride with care and be aware that you might need to get out of the way. It is only a 2km section before the buses turn off to reach the downhill trails. The exit from Elibank and Traquair Forest is on a nice, quiet path but it can be muddy in the wet so ride with care.

7 Once out of the forest, carry on to Traquair village, then head on to the B7062 past the impressive Traquair House (a white castle) and the famous bear gates.

8 A gravel track heads left off the road past some houses taking you on a scenic detour using the quiet tracks of Cardrona Forest. This is smooth gravel with fine valley views. Look out for horses, as it is a popular horse-riding forest.

9 Finally turn back on to the B7062 and head to Peebles for a well-deserved macaroni cheese pie from Forsyths.

Other routes or attractions in the area
Beyond the area's endless options for mountain biking and way-marked trails, the best gravel options to extend the riding are to the west on the Cross Borders Drove Road towards West Linton or, to the south, follow a track via Glenrath Hope in the Manor Valley and link into the gravel options around St Marys Loch. From the loch shores there are many forest track options heading south towards Craik Forest and Eskdalemuir.

05 THE HERRING ROADS OF THE LAMMERMUIRS
45KM/28 MILES

Introduction

This area is a real surprise gravel gem and a must-do ride in an area of Scotland that few tourists venture into. The Lammermuirs are a low, heather-clad moorland plateau near the east coast. This ride follows ancient traders' footsteps on the herring road routes across the hills. It is nearly all good quality gravel throughout the loop making it fast and fun.

The local area

The Lammermuirs are off the radar of most riders, even those relatively local to the area. The area offers a rolling expanse of upland terrain in the south-east of Scotland. It has an almost heathland feel to it, with sandy tracks and pockets of sparse pine forest. The start point is not far from some stunning beaches on the east coast and a spot of surfing can often be had making a full weekend away.

The area is famous for the herring roads which brought the fish inland from the villages along the East Lothian and Scottish Borders coastline. The actual routes of the ancient herring roads are hard to trace as they criss-crossed and migrated over the years, but this route follows a selection that gives you a feel for the paths which have been well-trodden by traders for centuries.

As a general rule, the area has a drier, warmer climate than the rest of Scotland, meaning it often avoids the worst Scottish weather. What the area is now most associated with, for better or worse, is wind turbines. It hosts the second largest inland wind farm in Scotland (at the time of writing at least!) and in any one

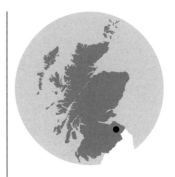

OPPOSITE THE INFAMOUS CAIRNS AT TWIN LAW.

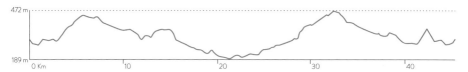

DISTANCE **45km/28 miles** — ASCENT **696m/2,283ft** — OFF-ROAD **67%**
START/FINISH **Minor road near Watch Water Reservoir, west of Longformacus**
START/FINISH GRID REF **NT 667560** — SATNAV **TD11 3PG**
GPS **55.7961, -2.5327** — MAP OS Landranger 73, Peebles, Galashiels & Selkirk; 74, Kelso & Coldstream (1:50,000)

GRAVEL SCALE

1 2 3 4 5

472 m

189 m

0 Km   10   20   30   40

GRAVEL RIDES SCOTLAND

direction it is likely they can be spotted. This also means new and well-surfaced gravel tracks have opened up but at the same time it has undoubtedly lost its wilderness feel and, in places, it's positively industrial with the pylons and associated substations.

Adding to the complex human relationship with the environment are the area's famous grouse shoots with the moorland management leaving zebra-like stripes of charred heather and frequent shooting butts like dimples on the landscape. However, if this all sounds a bit depressing, be reassured this route tells a story; it passes through some hidden valleys and the addition of an outstanding 'plateau-top' track combine to make it a firm favourite for in-the-know gravelleurs from nearby Edinburgh.

Early on, the route follows an eastern stretch of the Southern Upland Way to the summit of Twin Law. On this broad fell top, you'll find the two vast sprawling Twinlaw Cairns. According to legend, the cairns mark the graves of two brothers who fought on opposite sides in an ancient battle.

Route overview

The tracks are seemingly endless across this accessible wilderness, which made it hard to choose just one combination for this route and a place to start, so feel free to look at the map and pick and choose extra options.

This route was picked because it has a bit of every surface – from tarmac wind farm roads to short sections of singletrack that can be a bit muddy. The gravel varies from silky smooth to quite chunky, angular rocks that are rough but never get too big; a rating between 2 and 3 seems fair.

The most technical riding is around Twin Law with a singletrack climb that can be muddy in places. The descent after Twin Law is fast and fun but the puddles can be surprisingly deep and a bit muddy on the farm doubletrack. The route passes through a farmyard with some loud dogs; it is best to dismount and walk through and respect the responsible access. The climb up to the wind farm gets steep and rough in places, but once you are at the first turbine you are on well-maintained private wind farm roads and gravel tracks back to the start.

Navigation
The loop is best ridden clockwise from Watch Water Reservoir as the descents are generally more fun in this direction. Navigation is easier than many routes in the book because you are out in the open for the entire route, but an abundance of similar looking hill tracks combined with frequent low clouds can catch you out. Given the proximity to Edinburgh it is a surprisingly remote area; mobile reception varies from none at all to patchy.

Facilities and refreshments
There are no facilities at the start, nor along the route. The nearest options to the start are in Duns; you could extend the ride westwards over to Lauder for a variety of cafe and food shop options.

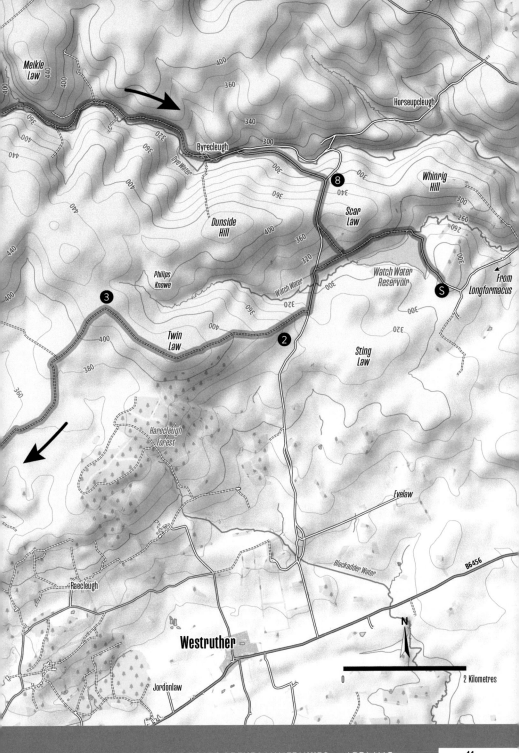

Meikle
Law

Horseupcleugh

Byrecleugh

Dye Water

Whinrig
Hill

8

Scar
Law

Dunside
Hill

Philips
Knowe

Watch Water
Reservoir

S

*From
Longformacus*

3

Twin
Law

2

Sting
Law

Watch Water

Harecleugh
Forest

Evelaw

Blackadder Water

B6456

Raecleugh

N

Westruther

Jordonlaw

0   2 Kilometres

BOTHY STOP WHILE EXPLORING (CANS OF CARLING WERE NOT THE AUTHOR'S!).

Bike shops

There are no bike shops close to the route. **Mikes Bikes** (T: 01620 825 931) in Haddington is probably the closest.

Public transport and access

This ride starts just east of Watch Water Reservoir – there is some informal parking towards the village of Longformacus. Be aware that the parking area at the reservoir itself is only for fishermen.

The nearest train station is too far away to be useful for a day ride; but the trains do open up options for a linear ride across the area, by starting at Dunbar and ending at Stow.

The route

S Head west on the minor road around Watch Water Reservoir. Pass through a farm to reach a new (tarmac) private road to access a wind farm. Turn left along this tarmac for a short section, then turn right on to grassy singletrack, following the sign for the *Southern Upland Way*.

2 The climb to Twin Law summit is steep but easily rideable in the dry on gravel tyres; traction on the mud can be challenging when wet. Enjoy the wide views from the plateau-like summit; take a picture of the cairns and have a rest on the stones before more gravel-bike-friendly singletrack heads downhill.

3 The Southern Upland Way takes a sharp left and on to a wider farm track. This can be very wet with huge, deep puddles if there's been much rain.

4 The next junction (where our route leaves the Southern Upland Way) is a right turn through a farmyard – it's best to walk through here and remember to be courteous, as you'll no doubt disturb some loud dogs as you pass through. After a short sharp climb from the farm the track is a bit rougher in a red colour rock before it descends from bleak moorland into a beautiful hidden glen with birch trees dotted along a fast-flowing stream called Earnscleugh Water.

GRAVEL RIDES SCOTLAND

ANOTHER TAKE ON THE CAIRNS AT TWIN LAW.

5 This valley track finally transitions into a smooth tarmac private road that serves a large house (marked as near Burncastle Lodge on OS maps) with a beautiful Victorian-style green-house. Continue on to reach the A697.

6 Turn right along the A697 then turn right along the next farm access road before Cleekhimin Bridge. Follow the road then fork right at Longcroft on to a track heading north-east. Avoid any tracks turning out of the steep-sided Whalplaw Glen; there is a ford to cross here and the track gets quite grassy before a steep climb up out of the glen.

7 At the head of the glen you'll see the wind turbines start and the tranquility is somewhat lost for the next section. Follow the main access road past the turbines and then past the vast substation. This tarmac wind farm road merges with a single-track public road. Ride for about 8km when you will reach the start of the tarmac private wind farm road you rode on earlier.

8 Fork right on to the road (this goes straight up and down the hill, presumably to avoid corners for the turbine deliveries). This tough, final climb sets you up a fast descent back to the reservoir. If you parked at the top of the hill, you'll regret it now, but it completes what is a fun little ride in a great corner of Scotland.

Other routes or attractions in the area

There are endless options for extending this route as tracks criss-cross the Lammermuirs – the most obvious option is carrying on north to extend this loop deeper into the Lammermuirs. For multi-day options either head east to the coast or west into the Southern Uplands and the Tweed Valley via the hill tracks above Lauder.

THE GRUELLING CLIMB UP TO
GLENLEITH FELL ON ROUTE 08.

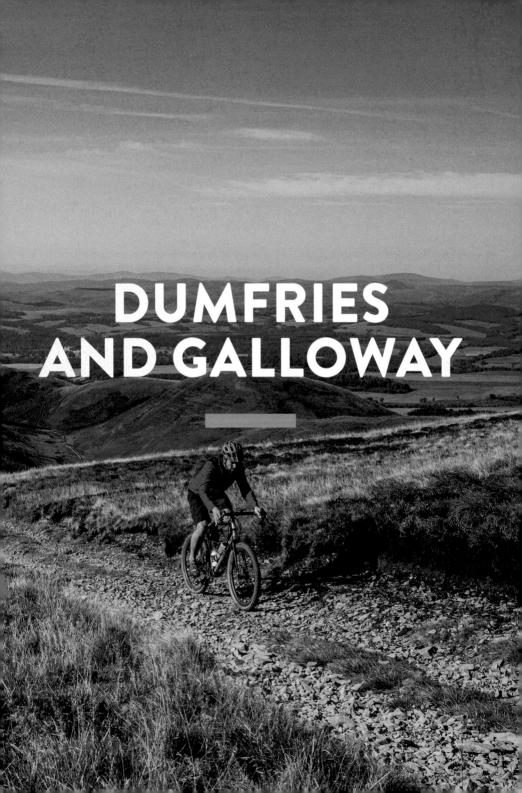

DUMFRIES
AND GALLOWAY

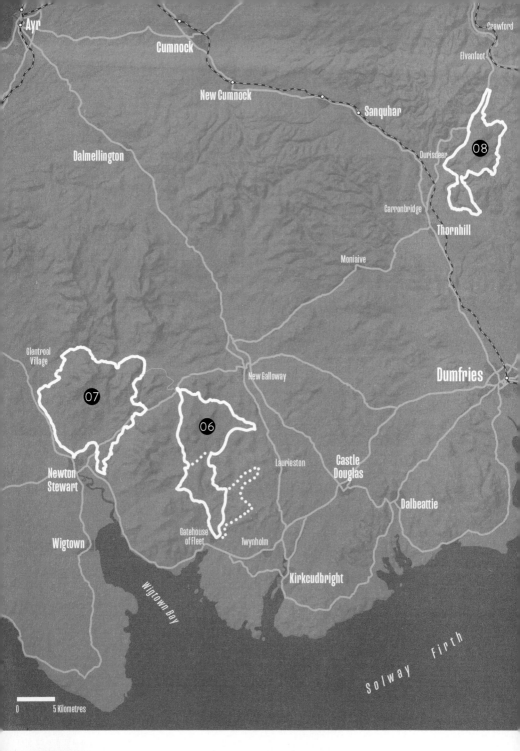

GRAVEL RIDES SCOTLAND

DUMFRIES AND GALLOWAY

Dumfries and Galloway is heaven for gravel lovers – it has a bit of everything and plenty of surprises. You'll find twisty coastal lanes, craggy hills and picturesque lochs that mirror the Lake District across the Solway Firth. Despite being so close to the Lake District you won't find crowded fells here. Dumfries and Galloway's reputation is growing as a real get-away-from-it-all place – somewhere peaceful to explore – and it really should be on all cyclists' bucket lists.

The region probably has the longest distance of gravel tracks per head of anywhere in the UK – some locals want it renamed as 'Dumfries and Gravelway'. These miles are through rich green, mossy plantation forest that suddenly break out to views over open hills or alongside peaceful wild-swim-friendly loch shores.

Away from the hills, the rich green pastures in the lowlands have lots of dairy farms; it is well worth a stop for an ice cream at the Cream o' Galloway dairy, or in the many cafes that stock it.

The routes selected here offer a variety of riding: **06 Gatehouse of Fleet** and **07 Galloway Forest Park Big Country Route** use smooth, well-maintained forest tracks, letting you ride hard and drift the corners. These contrast to **08 Daer Reservoir and Durisdeer**, which is on hill tracks and one of the most technically challenging rides in the book; it does reward you with huge views as you ride along a ridgetop track. The hills around Durisdeer are hugely underrated and the dramatic landscape so close to the A74(M) will make you ask why you've never been before.

06 **GATEHOUSE OF FLEET**
59KM/37 MILES

Introduction

A brilliant mix of quiet lanes and smooth gravel tracks, this ride heads under viaducts and on old railway lines, past otter pools on the river and along scenic forest drives. Gatehouse of Fleet is the perfect base and is rightly becoming a hub for cycling.

The local area

Gatehouse of Fleet sounds and looks like something out of a classic novel – it sits scenically on the Water of Fleet, with the Mill on the Fleet at one end of the High Street and an impressive clock tower at the other. The town is located beside a National Scenic Area with a wide range of gravel and road riding options. The town has lots of interesting little shops and the Mill on the Fleet visitor centre has a cafe and a bookshop with 20,000 books to choose from. To the south, it is not far to reach some great beaches with pleasant campsites, making it an ideal gravel riding minibreak.

Once you leave Gatehouse of Fleet you are soon in Cairnsmore of Fleet National Nature Reserve; there is a small car park here and the visitor centre has lots of information boards to learn more about the area. The Big Water of Fleet Viaduct can be seen from here, but remember the top is fenced off so you can't ride over it.

The ride uses sections of the now disused Portpatrick Railway, including a couple of impressive viaducts; you ride under the Big Water of Fleet Viaduct, but you can ride over the Stroan Viaduct, while enjoying great views over Stroan Loch and the surrounding forest. There are still remnants of an old station

OPPOSITE THE IMPRESSIVE BIG WATER OF FLEET VIADUCT NEAR GATEHOUSE OF FLEET.

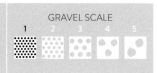

DISTANCE **59km/37 miles** — ASCENT **587m/1,926ft** — OFF-ROAD **60%**
START/FINISH **Gatehouse of Fleet** — START/FINISH GRID REF **NX 599562**
SATNAV **DG7 2HS** — GPS **54.8809, -4.1853** — MAP OS Landranger 77,
Dalmellington & New Galloway; 83, Newton Stewart & Kirkcudbright (1:50,000)

GRAVEL SCALE

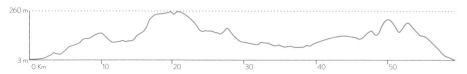

platform alongside the Portpatrick Railway path section, where the gravel is rough from the coarse stones that were under the original tracks.

On hot days the route offers a few wild swimming spots with multiple lochs and river pools, but it's probably best to avoid the rapids at the scenic Otter Pools. You're guaranteed to see an otter here (albeit wooden) before taking on the evocatively named Raiders' Road; the road inspired S. R. Crockett's *The Raiders*, which explores cattle reivers and general Borderlands intrigue.

Route overview

With no real killer climbs and the combination of peaceful lanes and smooth gravel, this is a good option for beginners. However, don't dismiss the 59 kilometres as 'easy'; it feels like more as there is over 500 metres of climbing. The route can easily be shortened; after about 13 kilometres you can head east, using a track parallel to the old Portpatrick Railway (although this is rougher than the main route and has some big puddles in wet weather), then rejoin the main route south-west of Loch Skerrow. (This shortcut is shown on the map and has a GPX file – **06a Gatehouse of Fleet: shortcut**, distance: 31 kilometres, ascent: 361 metres.)

The Raiders' Road is perfect fast gravel riding, but do watch out for cars on this public forest drive. The only rough bit of riding is the Portpatrick Railway path, which still has the coarse gravel from the trackbed. This section had a lot of forestry work in 2021 so was churned up in places, but should be regraded after the works finish. The route does make use of some quiet back roads; while not technically gravel these sections still suit gravel bikes well and offer high quality views across hills with some rollercoaster descents.

Navigation

The ride runs clockwise so it starts with a steady road climb alongside the Water of Fleet; riding in this direction also means a great descent to finish. Navigation can be a bit tricky in places because the back roads and forest tracks are confusing with a lot of turn offs. You do follow Sustrans National Route 7 markers until Clatteringshaws Loch, which helps, as does returning on the Raiders' Road forest drive.

Facilities and refreshments

Gatehouse of Fleet has a few nice cafes dotted around the town to relax and fuel up. **The Crafty Crow Cafe** in an old church on the High Street and the **Mill on the Fleet Cafe** are probably the best picks for good coffee.

There is a good range of accommodation options in the area, from B&Bs to traditional small hotels, and a nice selection of campsites on the Solway Coast; **Mossyard**, a campsite and caravan park on the beach near Gatehouse of Fleet, is recommended.

1 BEACH RIDING NEAR GATEHOUSE OF FLEET.

2 FUN RIDING NEAR THE BIG WATER OF FLEET VIADUCT.

3 GREAT VIEWS AND CHILD-FRIENDLY GRAVEL ON THE ADDITIONAL 06b LOOP.

4 MORE MESSING ABOUT ON THE BEACH POST RIDE.

5 EXAMPLE OF THE SMOOTH GRAVEL FOUND ON THE ROUTE.

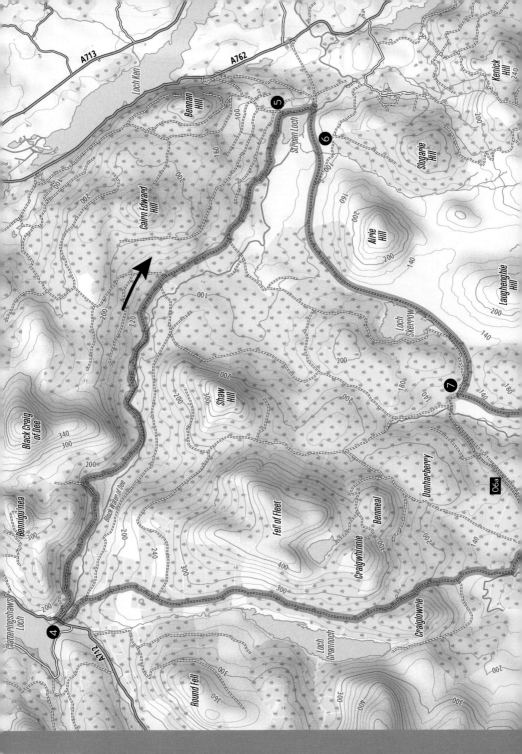

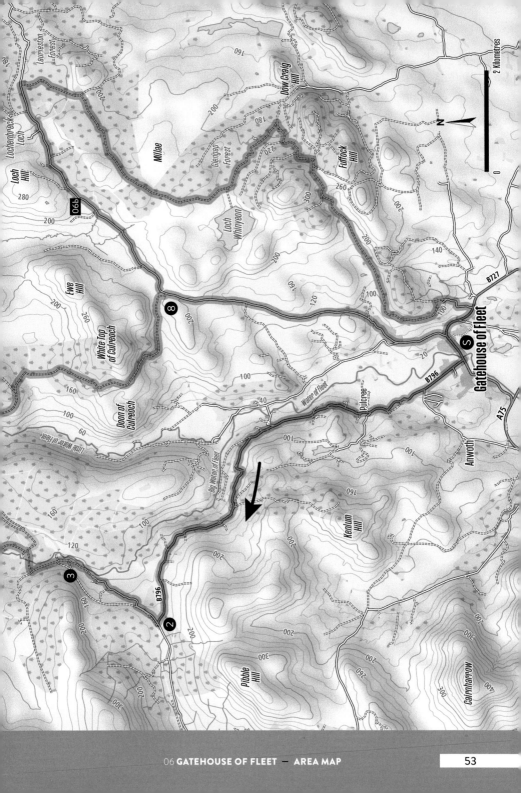

THE BIG WATER OF FLEET VIADUCT UP CLOSE.

Bike shops
Wheels of Fleet is a community cycling project tucked away behind the mill in Gatehouse of Fleet; while not a traditional bike shop, they are friendly and may be able to help out if open. They also have a few bikes available for hire. The next closest option is **The Break Pad** (T: 01671 401 303) at Kirroughtree Forest.

Public transport and access
Unless you are planning a long-distance ride you can't really access the area by public transport.

Parking is free in Gatehouse of Fleet; there are usually spaces in the main car park.

The route

S From the centre of Gatehouse of Fleet start a steady road climb on the B796, alongside the river. The first part of the route (until Clatteringshaws Loch) follows Sustrans National Route 7; the signposts are a useful navigational aid.

2 After about 10km, as the scenery opens up to reveal some stunning views, turn right at a T-junction. On this quiet, narrow lane descend towards Cairnsmore of Fleet National Nature Reserve; the old railway gravel track is visible on the left but don't be tempted to take it, as the viaduct is closed. This is initially tarmac but at the visitor centre car park it turns to a gravel track.

3 The next landmark is the impressive Big Water of Fleet Viaduct, a legacy of the abandoned Portpatrick Railway that the route picks up again later. The ride goes under an arch and will no doubt require a photo stop. Follow some sublime gravel forest tracks for about 12km to reach the A712 at Clatteringshaws Loch. (If your legs need a rest on a sunny day why not detour after about 8km for a quick dip in Loch Grannoch?)

4 You are now at the farthest point from the start. Turn right on to the A712 then turn right again, heading back east, on the Raiders' Road forest drive; this is yet more fantastic forest gravel but remember it is open to cars in both directions. Off to the side is

DRIFTWOOD FIRE ON THE BEACH BEFORE CAMPING.

a riverside picnic area called the Otter Pools, ideal for a lunch or snack stop. There is a large wooden otter to pretend with if the real ones are hiding; in my experience they usually are.

5 Continue on the Raiders' Road until you reach the scenic Stroan Loch and then the Stroan Viaduct. This is much smaller than the viaduct passed earlier, but you do get to ride over this one. You need to look carefully to find a gate and path at the back of the Stroan Viaduct car park on to the Portpatrick Railway path. There is a track under the arch that goes around and on to the railway, but it is much longer and rougher.

6 The Portpatrick Railway path is flat but alternates between smooth and coarse gravel, before ending at a T-junction.

7 At the T-junction some small yellow arrows point right for a local route; take the unsigned track on the left. Some fairly tiring ups and downs will test your stamina, but the lush green landscape with glimpses of the sea in the distance will keep you going.

8 Finally, turn right on the first tarmac road towards Gatehouse of Fleet. The final descent might not be gravel but it's a great piece of riding on any bike. Stop for a coffee and cake in town to finish a great day out.

Other routes or attractions in the area

For those who want to avoid the last section of tarmac or those who think 59 kilometres is too short, the ride can be extended to the east on more gravel tracks. It takes you through more forests and past more lochs, ending on a gravel track just outside of Gatehouse of Fleet. This extension is shown on the map and has a GPX file – **06b Gatehouse of Fleet: extension**, distance: 74 kilometres, ascent: 758 metres.

Sustrans National Route 7 runs through the area – this section is a classic gravel ride. This goes west past Clatteringshaws Loch and links into **07 Galloway Forest Park Big Country Route** (pages 57–63). For most riders this means an overnight stop; White Laggan Bothy (owned by the Mountain Bothies Association) is just off the track, but it isn't the nicest bothy, so take your camping kit as a backup. There really are just so many great bikepacking options in this area.

GALLOWAY FOREST PARK BIG COUNTRY ROUTE
64KM/40 MILES

Introduction

If Galloway is a must-go gravel destination, then this route is the classic ride. It feels like a real journey. Starting in the forest, it heads out to take in lochs, craggy hills, modern sculptures, historic monuments, open views and even some optional easy mountain bike descents.

The local area

This route is based on the waymarked 7stanes Big Country Route around Galloway Forest Park, but with an added bonus and a different start point (it traditionally starts at Glentrool). This ride is mile-munching fast on easy gravel but with the option to add in some more technical riding too. It travels through what is undoubtedly the biggest scenery in South West Scotland.

The 7stanes are seven forests across the south of Scotland each with MTB trails. *Stane* is a Scottish word for stone and each location has a unique sculpture of some kind, varying from a meteorite to large carved inscriptions. The Glentrool sculpture is based on the legends of Scottish and Irish giants throwing things at each other – the 1.5-ton sculpture overlooking Loch Dee is designed to look like a Neolithic stone axe head and has some runic text on it to decipher too.

The most prominent sight along the way is Murray's Monument, standing proud on the hill near Black Loch. This giant needle was erected in 1835 in honour of Alexander Murray, a local shepherd who became Professor of Oriental Languages at the University of Edinburgh. On the shores of Loch Black, look out for a similar

OPPOSITE THE PRIMO GRAVEL RIDING TO BE FOUND IN KIRROUGHTREE FOREST.

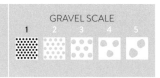

DISTANCE **64km/40 miles** ― ASCENT **966m/3,169ft**
OFF-ROAD **70%** ― START/FINISH **Kirroughtree Visitor Centre**
START/FINISH GRID REF **NX 452648** ― SATNAV **DG8 7BE**
GPS **54.9537, -4.4189** ― MAP **OS Landranger 77, Dalmellington & New Galloway; 83, Newton Stewart & Kirkcudbright (1:50,000)**

GRAVEL SCALE
1 2 3 4 5

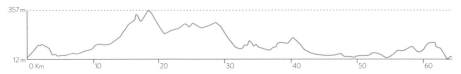

357 m

12 m

0 Km   10   20   30   40   50   60

needle – this is a smaller sculpture commissioned by Forestry Commission Scotland in the late 1990s.

Around the corner is a Wild Goat Park in what feels like a very random location, but this nature reserve is home to a herd of British primitive goats; these animals are descendants of the first domesticated goats who were introduced to the British Isles around 5,000 years ago. After looking for goats, have a look in the sky, as soaring red kites are a very common sight.

Route overview

This route is probably one of the very finest long-distance gravel loops in the UK. The 7stanes Big Country Route might have been originally marketed as a mountain bike ride, but it should be rebranded as a gravel route because it is textbook gravel riding. This route is given a rating of 1, as the tracks are pretty much all smooth and well surfaced with no notably bad sections.

Within Kirroughtree you ride past the infamous McMoab, a section of large humpback granite rocks named after the iconic Moab Slickrock Trail in Utah. The young trees are growing up fast around the trail, so you'll need to look carefully to spot it. It is verging on trial riding, and on a gravel bike you'll bang the bottom bracket a lot attempting the techy bits!

As you return to Kirroughtree Forest near the end of the ride you can opt to detour on to a signposted blue/red graded mountain bike descent; while it's actually pretty rough and verging on unpleasant on drop bars, undoubtedly some riders will like the challenge to end the route.

Of course, you could just roll up at Glentrool and ride the standard waymarked Big Country Route, but this version mixes it up with some singletrack options and more great gravel riding. Kirroughtree is also easier to access than Glentrool for most visitors.

Navigation

The route has to be ridden anticlockwise, because it uses official waymarked mountain bike trails. This direction also lets you navigate more easily using the purple arrow waymarkers of the Big Country Route.

As the Big Country Route is waymarked, there is limited navigation required; however, within Kirroughtree Forest it can be confusing and it's actually quite easy to end up back where you started if you're not careful. You can relax once you pick up the purple arrow waymarkers for the Big Country Route at Black Loch.

Facilities and refreshments

Starting at Kirroughtree means a huge car park, toilets with showers, a well-stocked bike shop, **Kirroughtree Cafe** and two small play parks for young kids. The other options are starting in the nearby town of Newton Stewart or at Glentrool Visitor Centre. Newton Stewart has food and drink options aplenty including award-winning gin at **Crafty Distillery** – it's worth a stop (post ride!). **Glentrool Visitor Centre** is just off this route but has a seasonal cafe with toilets.

OPPOSITE CLASSIC LOG PILE RIDING SHOT FROM KIRROUGHTREE.

1 THE TOWERING NEEDLE OF MURRAY'S MONUMENT. **2** WATCH OUT FOR THE BIG COUNTRY LOOP WAYMARKERS.

Bike shops
The Break Pad (T: 01671 401 303) at Kirroughtree Forest is well stocked and has experienced mechanics. **Kirkcowan Cycles** (T: 01671 401 529) in Newton Stewart is also useful.

Public transport and access
The nearest station is at Barrhill which is around 17km to the west and can be linked in with gravel tracks for most of the distance.

Parking at Kirroughtree Forest is pay and display – you'll need a full day there, but with a cafe, showers and a bike shop it is very handy.

The route

S From Kirroughtree Visitor Centre, ride out to the trailhead starting at the left of the cafe. However, don't follow the singletrack trails; the ride follows the gravel track which the waymarked MTB routes cut back and forth across as they traverse the forest.

2 The track undulates until you reach a right turn on to a tarmac forestry road. This takes you in a fast descent until an obvious left turn returns you on to gravel. Follow this track but don't be tempted to divert on to the red or black MTB singletrack; generally all these sections are too rough for gravel bikes.

3 The track climbs up to the infamous McMoab section of the Kirroughtree black MTB route, a section of slick granite rock requiring skill and balance – you can try it on a gravel bike, but it will take Danny MacAskill skill levels! The track leaves Kirroughtree and reaches the A712 (also known as The Queen's Way); on the hill in front is the imposing Murray's Monument. Turn right on to the A712, passing the Wild Goat Park before you turn left towards Black Loch.

4 At the end of the scenic Black Loch pick up the purple arrow waymarkers of the Big Country Route and follow these for the next 42km.

PERFECT GRAVEL LIKE THIS IS THE HALLMARK OF THIS LOOP.

5 Pass Loch Dee and then Loch Trool. Just after Loch Trool turn left, still following the purple arrow waymarkers (Glentrool Visitor Centre is straight ahead here).

6 Just after passing through the outskirts of Newton Stewart, turn right on to a small back lane (leaving the Big Country Route). Turn right again on to the A712.

7 From the A712 take the next left turn signposted *Glenamour Forest car park*. This takes you into the back of Kirroughtree Forest. Once in the forest, turn right twice to follow the main track.

8 Decision time comes when you see a sign for the *The Rocky Road* singletrack section on the blue and red waymarked MTB trails. This descent is very bumpy in places but generally drop-bar-friendly if your skills and bike allow; it will eventually take you all the way back to Kirroughtree Visitor Centre. If some mountain biking doesn't appeal, keep on the gravel track down to the paved back road that leads to Kirroughtree Visitor Centre to complete the loop.

Other routes or attractions in the area

This loop has far too many add-on options with tracks heading in every direction. The best recommendation is the Sustrans National Route 7 which heads east to Clatteringshaws Loch and then on to Gatehouse of Fleet (linking with **06 Gatehouse of Fleet** (pages 49–55)). Sustrans National Route 7 keeps going east, but it is best to head off north on a local waymarked cycle route towards the Forest of Ae, where there is a great waymarked gravel track through to the nice little town of Moffat.

DAER RESERVOIR AND DURISDEER
51KM/32 MILES

Introduction

This route follows ridgetop tracks offering some of the highest gravel riding in this book, but there's a catch – you have to get up to the ridge. The riding is all on gravel tracks, but it is probably the second most rough and technical route in this book. Luckily the rewards are evident when you get to the top!

The local area

The Lowther Hills are the steepest and highest fells in Dumfries and Galloway; covering a relatively small area, they are easily overlooked and rarely visited, which is baffling as they are simply stunning. When the sun is shining the area around Durisdeer feels like a peaceful little paradise, with views of lakes and distant fells meaning it is reminiscent of the nearby Lake District. In bad weather, with rain driving against the small, white and lonely Scottish cottages, it reminds you how dramatic and high this route can get – it is not a place to be taken lightly in adverse conditions. Meeting another soul on these tracks who isn't a farmer feels almost suspicious, such is the isolation.

The climbs are steep and loose, but the reward is a ridgetop track with a 360-degree panorama over the bigger hills of Galloway, Drumlanrig Castle (another epic holiday home of the Duke of Buccleuch) and across the Solway coastline. This is the area where *The Thirty-Nine Steps*, the famous John Buchan spy novel, was set; for those unfamiliar with the story, a fugitive gets the train here and goes on the run for days – something you can easily imagine when you see the emptiness.

OPPOSITE THE STEEP BUT REWARDING CLIMB OUT OF DURISDEER.

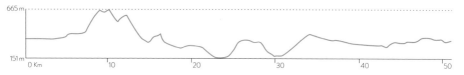

DISTANCE **51km/32 miles** — ASCENT **1,091m/3,579ft** — OFF-ROAD **80%**
START/FINISH **Daer Reservoir** — START/FINISH GRID REF **NS 974086**
SATNAV **ML12 6TJ** — GPS **55.3607, -3.6200** — MAP **OS Landranger 78, Nithsdale & Annandale (1:50,000)**

GRAVEL SCALE

1   2   3   4   **5**

665 m

151 m

0 Km   10   20   30   40   50

GRAVEL RIDES SCOTLAND

Route overview

This route is a lot of fun in a remarkable area and, while it is all on tracks or roads, it does push the limit of gravel riding in two sections. From Kirkhope at the southern end of Daer Reservoir the track starts off well, but you'll almost certainly be off the bike and pushing for sections up Shiel Dod. The ridge provides some lovely riding and is well worth saving for a clear, sunny day. The descent down Glenleith Fell is technical – it is on boulder gravel and needs some skill to ride all the way. Once down this descent you can briefly relax before the next steep descent past the concerningly named Bishop Holes; the track slowly fades away as you head along Garroch Water to the road. The stand-out feature here is the number of burn crossings – wet feet are guaranteed. From the road the route is now almost all on good stone tracks and beautiful quiet road riding.

Given the conditions and the elevation, make sure you allow more time for the distance than for your average gravel ride. The direct A702 climb option back up towards Daer Reservoir is great road riding, but this route takes the stony track north from Durisdeer to keep to the theme of underbiking. You might opt for suspension if possible.

The burn crossings on the Garroch Water track do need caution; if the burns are in spate they can get deep. If you want to avoid this section, you can cut across to Durisdeer on good farm tracks. Whichever bike you decide to take, you'll love the views across a remote pocket of Scotland that has a few surprises in store.

Navigation

Riding clockwise makes the climbs more achievable and means more climbing is on the road. There are a few tracks in these hills; the section through the forest back to Daer Reservoir needs careful navigating. The ridgetop is exposed and while lovely in sunshine would be quickly disorientating in bad weather.

Facilities and refreshments

The route is completely without facilities and has very patchy mobile reception. For those wanting a coffee or food afterwards, the town of Thornhill is only a short detour from the southern tip of the route and could work as an alternative start point. Otherwise, you'll have to take the next motorway services in either direction.

OPPOSITE DEFINITE TYPE 2 FUN UP TO GLENLEITH FELL.

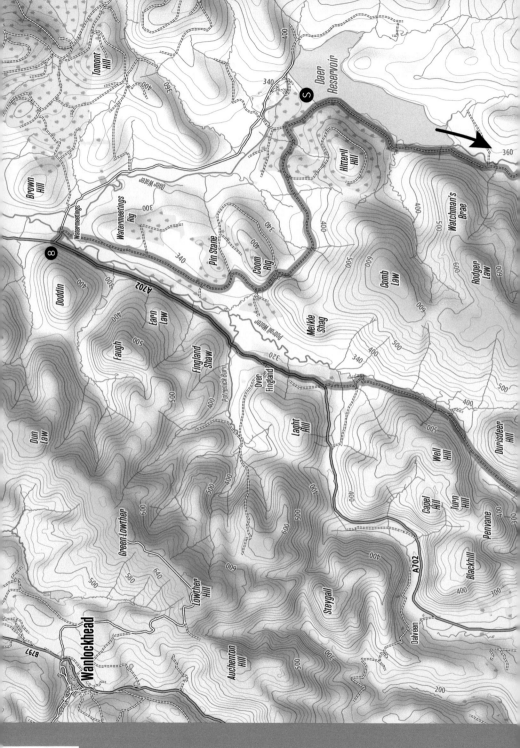

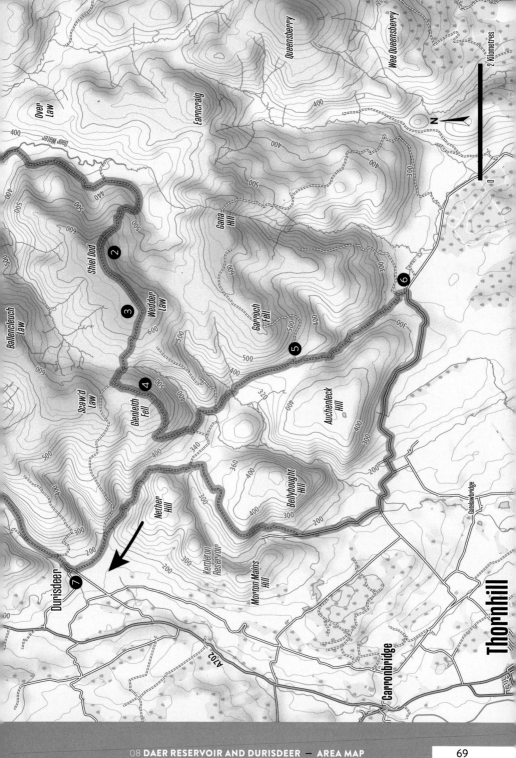

DAER RESERVOIR FISHING PERMITS REQUIRED!

Ae Forest Bike Shop & Cafe (T: 01387 860 805) is a bit of a way from the route, but a good option if you're heading that way.

Public transport and access
There are no practical public transport options.

The easiest access point is to start at Daer Reservoir (where there is some informal roadside parking), which is just a stone's throw from the A74(M). Don't let this make you think you are close to civilization, as the hum of motorway traffic is quickly left behind. Durisdeer is a quaint little village; it is on one of the lowest points of the route and is often the starting point for mountain bike routes. There is some limited parking in Durisdeer and in lay-bys on the relatively quiet A702, but Daer Reservoir is the best bet.

The route

S Head south along the side of Daer Reservoir – it is on good tarmac and a great warm-up. The gravel track starts shortly after the water ends at Kirkhope; it is easy to navigate and smooth going for a few kilometres. You'll pass a few gates and cross a well-constructed bridge along the way.

2 Then the climbing begins up to Shiel Dod with a steep, loose section, which for most people means a push uphill. The following section is still uphill but rideable before the final, steep section to the summit means more time off the bike and pushing towards the broad ridge. You might not believe it, but riding in this direction means the steep sections of climb are shorter than the other direction. Once on the top of Shiel Dod, stop and enjoy the sweeping views of the mountains; wind turbines dot the landscape with Wintercleuch Fell and the vast Clyde Wind Farm in the distance.

3 A gentle climb brings you to Wedder Law before a sharp descent and climb takes you south to Glenleith Fell. From this western end of the ridge you can enjoy views of Galloway set behind Drumlanrig Castle; keep watching the skies as red kites will likely be sweeping about.

A DIFFERENT VIEW OF A SHEEP PEN WHILE HEADING WEST FROM DAER RESERVOIR.

④ The descent from Glenleith Fell is steep and loose and needs care. Turn left, ford the Glenleith Burn (which is okay but needs taking slowly) then start a climb on a decent, but old, track to slowly regain the next high point.

⑤ The descent along and across Garroch Water gets vague and it is rough in places; eventually you cross a bridge to reach a minor road.

⑥ Turn right and follow the quiet back road before taking a track heading north towards Kettleton Reservoir; it climbs up steeply on better gravel. Continue along the track to reach Durisdeer.

⑦ From Durisdeer you have two equally scenic options. Either, as is shown on the map and GPX file, take the track north out of Durisdeer (this is generally in good condition but sees little farm traffic meaning it is slowly grassing over at time of writing) then head north on the A702 – or enjoy the full A702 road climb, which is very dramatic but can have a steady stream of fast cars whizzing past.

⑧ Turn right on to the road leading towards Daer Reservoir, then turn right to follow forest tracks back to the reservoir.

Other routes or attractions in the area

From the southern end of the loop you can go south-east on the road for 10 kilometres to the Forest of Ae to explore an extra gravel loop and the cafe here. You can keep riding on a local waymarked cycle route through the Forest of Ae towards Beattock. Either add this to a huge loop following a cycle route alongside the A74(M) before cutting across the forest to Daer Reservoir and rejoining the main route or make it a linear route ending at Moffat, where there are some good cafes.

IT'S ALWAYS T SHIRT WEATHER ON THE SCENIC
LOCH ECK LOOP (ROUTE 09).

ARGYLL AND BUTE

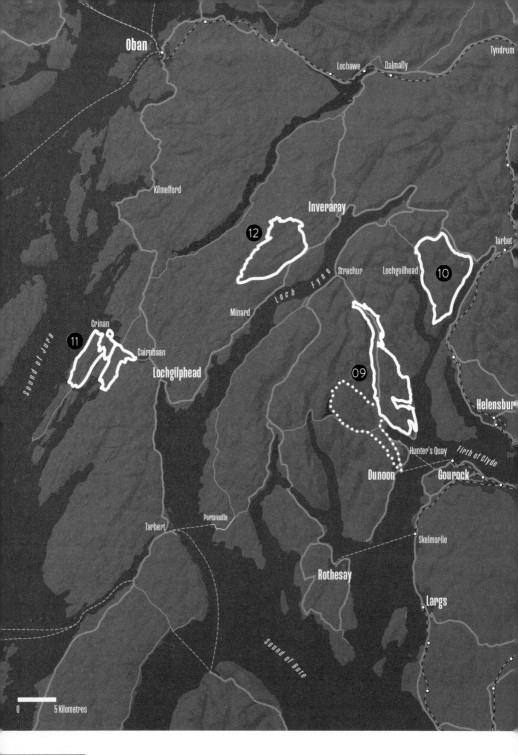

ARGYLL AND BUTE

—

Argyll is well tucked away on the west coast and, to be honest, it can be a bit of a drag to get to if you live further away than Glasgow; however, maybe because of this, it is a surprise to find such a gravel gem of a destination. Expect wild, rocky coastlines with fingers between sea lochs and inlets, rising into rich green mossy forests below craggy peaks. This is the west coast so it does rain here, and the lushness of the landscape will really hit you while the weather adds to the drama.

On a warm summer's weekend, it feels alpine with the steep mountains, large lochs and the wild flower meadows breaking out of the forests. While exploring the area for this book it really did deliver more than expected on so many levels. The west coast midges can be fierce, but don't let that put you off a visit in midsummer, as there is often enough breeze to keep them away.

For lovers of seafood, the area is rightly famous for salmon and oysters – it has a great selection of restaurants including Loch Fyne Oysters at Clachan and the delightful Samphire in Inveraray. Wild About Argyll has some really useful information about the attractions of the area, as well as details of a long-distance bikepacking route, which is a combination of road, gravel and a few more technical mountain bike sections.

09 LOCH ECK AND LOCH LONG
58KM/36 MILES

Introduction

This is an adventurous gravel route that will surprise you with its variety of rich forests, magnificent views of Loch Eck, Beinn Mhòr and even the west coast islands of Jura and Islay. On a sunny midsummer's day, the views down Loch Eck are reminiscent of alpine lakes with the steep craggy peaks and flower-filled meadows above the treeline.

The local area

The geography of Argyll and Bute, and this area in particular, is confusing with so many peninsulas and sea lochs making it hard to comprehend what is connected to where. It is also hard to reach, making it notably quieter compared to other beautiful parts of Scotland.

This ride is all about the wild landscape and the forests. The area is the heart of the Argyll Forest Park, a huge forested area that is mostly plantations of Sitka spruce trees, but it also has many pockets of large deciduous trees through to monstrous redwoods which this route rides under.

Glenbranter is the start point of the route and one of the jewels in the crown of Argyll Forest Park; the area has a fantastic old oak forest and a great mossy gorge walk. It was one of the first areas to be planted in the 1920s and is scattered with stunning rhododendrons too.

Just before Ardentinny, up a short sharp gravel climb, you'll ride past the Lairds Grave – a lonely grave site between two large yew trees and surrounded by large fir trees with views of Loch Long.

OPPOSITE THE VIEW DOWN OVER LOCH ECK HAS AN ALPINE FEEL.

DISTANCE **58km/36 miles** ━ ASCENT **1,205m/3,953ft** ━ OFF-ROAD **75%**
START/FINISH **Glenbranter, at the northern end of Loch Eck**
START/FINISH GRID REF **NS 112976** ━ SATNAV **PA27 8DJ**
GPS **56.1337, -5.0397** ━ MAP OS Landranger 56, Loch Lomond & Inveraray; 63, Firth of Clyde (1:50,000)

GRAVEL SCALE
1 2 3 4 5

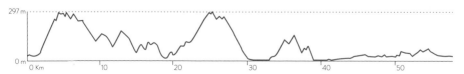

A REAL WOW FACTOR VIEW ACROSS THE BUSY FIRTH OF CLYDE.

Navigation

This route is best ridden in a clockwise direction due to a few nicer descents and getting the big climb done early on in the ride; the flat blast along Loch Eck is the ideal way to end the ride. The route isn't the hardest to navigate as it follows lochs and the coastline, but is a long and committing route so a wrong turn can have bigger consequences.

Halfway around the route is the Argyll Mausoleum, next to St Munn's Church. It is the resting place of the Dukes and Earls of Argyll and loaded with historical significance. Prior to this it was the Campbell Clan burial ground; it is also located on the concerningly named Midge Lane! Kilmun Arboretum is another remarkable forest, signposted off the route as you pass Kilmun on the southern coastal section. There is nowhere quite like it in Scotland; the forestry commission used it as a test site and planted over 260 types of trees. Many didn't like the Scottish weather (and maybe the midges too); however, many did survive, and the temperate climate means they grew even bigger than they might have done in their native climates.

The next stop just off the route for those with time to kill is Puck's Glen, an amazing dark ravine that is rich in moss and ferns – a walk into another magical world. With waterfalls and plunge pools it is nice on a hot day to cool off. It contains a lot of steps so unfortunately isn't bike-friendly.

Towards the end of the ride, Benmore Botanic Garden is remarkable for its towering giant conifers and rhododendrons. There is an entry fee to visit the gardens and there is a cafe (check opening hours before you go); it is well worth a visit while in the area.

1 FOXGLOVES LINE THE ROUTE IN SUMMER. 2 THE DARK MOSSY FOREST DAPPLED IN SUNLIGHT.

Route overview

This ride gets the big climbs out the way early and finishes with a flat and fast blast alongside Loch Eck. The first climb starts from the A815 leading up to sweeping views and on to a great descent that's a bit loose in places but just seems to go on and on. The full route is mostly on superb gravel tracks. In particular, the added horseshoe section around Stronchullin Burn near Blairmore Hill is gravel bike perfection with the track curving out enticingly ahead on both sides of the glen. The ride back north alongside Loch Eck after Benmore Botanic Garden is scenic and a real pedal-to-the-metal gravel grind – it is a great way to finish, especially with a prevailing tailwind.

There are very short hike-a-bikes on paths between Loch Eck and Ardentinny; these techy sections do mix it up with a nice challenge for those that enjoy it. However, you can clearly identify them on the OS map and detour around by staying on the road between Loch Eck and Ardentinny; the section of note is at grid reference NS 171897.

With so many options in this area it was hard to pin down a final route, but this is a cracker, taking in a lot of the area's attractions while on superb textbook gravel.

Facilities and refreshments

On the first half of the route there are no services, but there is a handy petrol station shop and the American-inspired **Sheila's Diner** on the A815 at Ardbeg (sadly not home to Ardbeg Whisky).

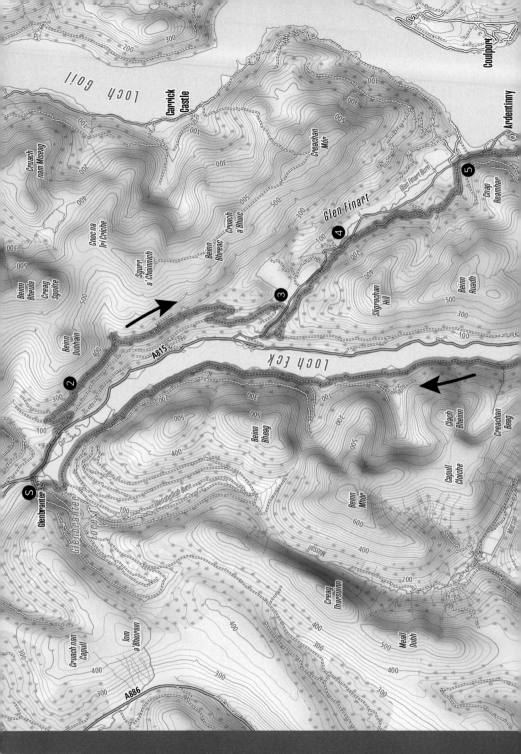

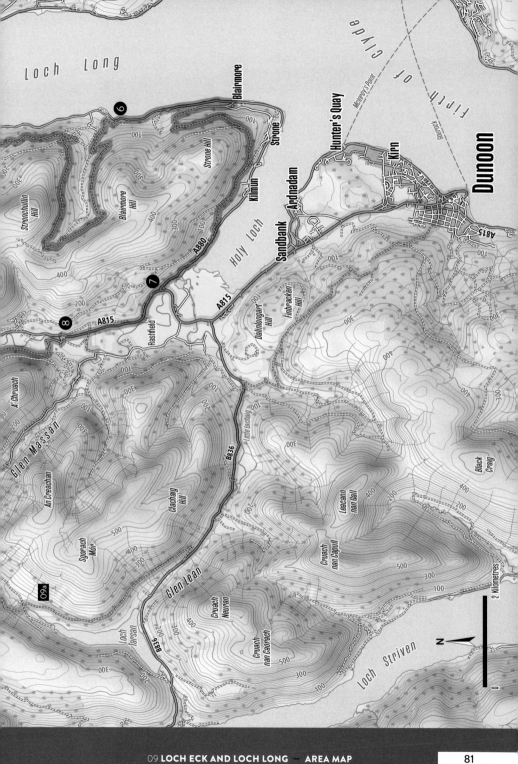

THE START OF THE FAST AND FUN DESCENT TO GLEN FINART.

Bike shops
Start Line MTB Dunoon
(T: 07733 303 359) do bike
hire and repairs.

Public transport and access
Free parking is available at the
start of the route at Glanbranter.

A few kilometres to the south
of the route is Dunoon, which
is accessible via ferry from
Gourock, just to the west of
Glasgow. For many coming from
the south it is easier to catch
the ferry rather than driving
round to reach Glenbranter,
but for one-off car trips it is
quite expensive. A good option
is to get the train to Gourock
then catch the ferry as a foot
passenger to Dunoon for a
weekend, or even a day ride –
the bonus is bikes are free to
take on the ferry.

The route

S From Glenbranter, head out on to the A815 and turn right.
After 1km turn left on to a gravel track (following a signpost
for the *Loch Eck Loop*); the climb starts immediately with some
hairpins to negotiate.

2 The climb does eventually level out, leaving the treeline behind
– in summer the landscape has an alpine feel with meadows full
of wild flowers and views across the loch. A group of masts and
aerials signal the high point before a long, fast and fun descent
back through the forest.

3 As you join the narrow back road you can either turn right and
then left on to a fun gravel section (as shown on the map and in
the GPX file) or turn left along the road, missing out this gravel
section. The gravel section is proper fast gravel riding; a small
section of it is part of the waymarked Loch Eck Loop.

4 The track comes down to meet the road before peeling away
again. This signals the start of the next grass-down-the-middle
gravel climb. (You can opt to stay on the road here, avoiding
the roughest gravel of the route, and rejoin the route further
east at Loch Long.) This climb is on doubletrack into a dark,
mossy tunnel through the forest. Finally, the track ends and
there's a short section of path that is steep and involves some
hike-a-bike. This links two tracks together and is only short,
but it is getting overgrown. It is rideable in places and overall
it is worth the short pain from pushing. Careful navigating is
required in this forest as some new tracks have been completed
since the OS maps were last updated.

MORE VIEWS OF LOCH ECK LOOKING SOUTH.

5 Return to the road briefly then turn off uphill again (at a signpost for *Lairds Grave*). Stay on the main track and hairpin up to the Blairmore gravel horseshoe – a loop around a glen that offers views out to Loch Long but also across to the mouth-watering tracks that you will ride down on the other side.

6 Return to the road again, this time along the loch shore, before another gravel climb takes you up to epic views over the confluence of four lochs and across to Dunoon, with sailing boats and ferries dotting the water. The track heads downhill again to the coast; it slowly deteriorates before passing through what looks like someone's garden and on to the A880. Turn right along the road, passing St Munn's Church and Kilmun Arboretum.

7 Reach a junction where the A880 meets the A815. Here you can either turn right to stay on the main route, heading for Benmore Botanic Garden, or you can turn left to add in an extra loop to Loch Tarsan. (This alternative route forms part of the GPX file **09a Loch Eck and Loch Long: alternative start and extension** – it is all well surfaced and offers more breathtaking views.)

8 Turn left on to the track heading around the edge of Benmore Botanic Garden then join the gravel track around Loch Eck. Follow the shoreline and head back to Glenbranter and be grateful for the lack of climbing and smooth surface all the way back!

Other routes or attractions in the area
A GPX file of a longer route with Dunoon as a start point is available (**09a Loch Eck and Loch Long: alternative start and extension**, distance: 91 kilometres, ascent: 1,639 metres), so you can get the ferry to Dunoon from near Glasgow. Or you can make the route linear and keep heading north, either heading for Oban railway station or, for a shorter option, towards Arrochar and Tarbet railway station.

10 THE DUKES PATH, LOCHGOILHEAD AND THE ARROCHAR ALPS
32KM/20 MILES

Introduction

A short sharp Argyll classic that is mostly on smooth gravel. However, The Dukes Path singletrack section is steep and rough in places, and at 4 kilometres it is the longest section of techy singletrack riding in this book.

The local area

This ride is about the atmospheric forests but also the challenge of riding a gravel bike down The Dukes Path, which many riders will find fun, but some will curse! It is also about the lochside views and the sheer drama of riding with views over to The Cobbler, an iconic rocky mountain in the Arrochar Alps.

Lochgoilhead is a long way from anywhere, but this ride takes you past this village and its dramatic setting. Steep hills on all sides converge to a sea loch with sweeping views. The area was first settled near where you might spot Carrick Castle on the western shore of Loch Goil. The castle was originally built in the thirteenth century, though the ruins visible today date back to a tower house built in the fifteenth century. The village only really existed due to the steamers from the Clyde calling here as a holiday destination. As you look across today it is mostly cabins and caravan sites. However, you'll also see lots of tantalising gravel tracks heading west and south too.

Near the end of the ride, you get views over the infamous Rest and be Thankful road. This section of the A83 follows one of General Wade's classic military roads built in 1750. It isn't hard to imagine troops marching along it through the green, misty glen,

OPPOSITE VIEWS ACROSS TO THE WONDERFUL SETTING OF LOCHGOILHEAD.

DISTANCE **32km/20 miles** — ASCENT **769m/2,523ft** — OFF-ROAD **90%**
START/FINISH **Coilessan car park, south of Ardgartan, Loch Long**
START/FINISH GRID REF **NN 259011** — SATNAV **G83 7AR**
GPS **56.1707, -4.8058** — MAP **OS Landranger 56, Loch Lomond**
& Inveraray (1:50,000)

GRAVEL SCALE

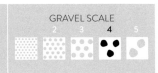

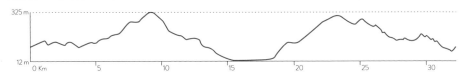

GRAVEL RIDES SCOTLAND

nor to imagine the herds of cattle from when the route was previously used as an old drovers' route. It is now, unfortunately, more famous for being on the traffic news following yet another landslide closing it for a prolonged period. At the head of Glen Croe is a stone inscribed with 'Rest and be Thankful', as weary travellers would say when they've made it to the top. Given the gravel climb to this view, you'll no doubt see the bench in the forest near here and say the same.

Route overview

It might not surprise you to hear that this is an old school classic mountain bike ride, drawing riders in with the short Dukes Path singletrack section. But, considering it is 4 kilometres of single-track with the remaining 28 kilometres on tracks, it is well suited to experienced gravelleurs.

The route direction is clockwise; on paper this looks obvious because you descend the techy Dukes Path singletrack section when travelling in this direction. There is only one other section of singletrack above Ardgartan, which crosses a gorge on a bridge so needs a dismount up and around before a very short techy descent. The rest of the route is on fast, smooth gravel – it is pure gravel riding at its best. Some may opt to ride the route in an anticlockwise direction – taking the pain and enduring a hike-a-bike up The Dukes Path and then enjoying the remainder as fast gravel descents.

Beware of the track climbing up Gleann Mòr towards Rest and be Thankful; while it is well maintained it is a long climb, and for some reason there can often be cars on it. However, despite its MTB past, with such a short section of singletrack and so much prime gravel, this route deserves its place on the list of the great gravel rides of Scotland.

Navigation

The route direction described here is clockwise, because you might prefer to descend the techy Dukes Path singletrack section. As a loop that follows defined glens it is relatively easy to navigate. The Dukes Path cycle route is signposted, but the marked route involves a different and rougher section of singletrack, so don't blindly follow them.

The track through the forest opposite Rest and be Thankful is straightforward; make sure that you don't turn left off it or you'll drop too low.

Facilities and refreshments

There is a small cafe on the **Ardgartan Forest Holidays** site, but it's mostly aimed at residents staying there. For more food and drink options you are not far from Arrochar at the start, which has better options. Although cycling on this section of the A83 to reach Arrochar is not recommended, there is a steep path and track off-road link.

You can also start or just call into Lochgoilhead which is in a dramatic and very isolated spot on the shore of Loch Goil – there is a car park, a small post office shop and **The Goil Inn** with basic pub-style food and drink options.

There are accommodation options all over the area from campsites and hotels in Lochgoilhead to the holiday lodges at Ardgartan.

OPPOSITE THE INFAMOUS DUKES PATH ROUTE IS NOW SIGNPOSTED.

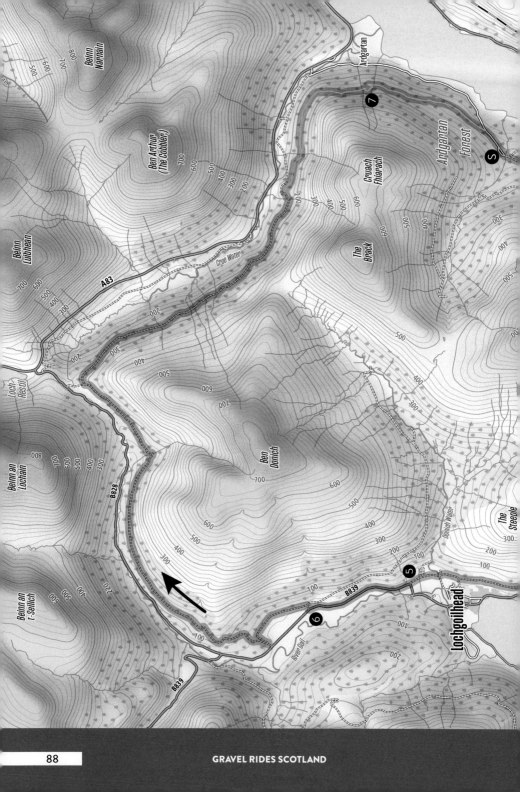

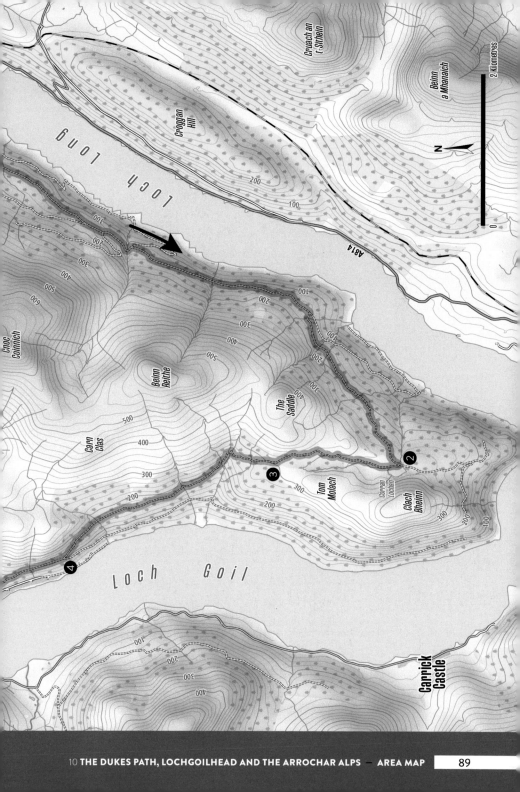

Loch Long

Cruach an t-Sithein

Beinn a Mhanaich

Croggan Hill

2 Kilometres

N

A814

200

100

100

200

300

400

500

600

Cnoc Coinnich

Beinn Reithe

The Saddle

100

200

300

400

200

300

Carn Clas

500

400

300

200

300

300

Tom Molach

Corran Lochain

Clach Bheinn

200

100

③

④

Loch Goil

100

200

300

400

Carrick Castle

②

THE DUKES PATH SINGLETRACK STARTS HERE – GET READY FOR SOME BUMPS.

Bike shops
Campbell Bike Workshop
(T: 07811 123 943) is based at
Mansefield Studios in Arrochar.

Public transport and access
Arrochar and Tarbet railway
station is located between
Arrochar and Tarbet and makes
this loop accessible by train.
   This route starts at a forest
car park just south of the
Ardgartan Forest Visitor Centre,
which is signed from the A83.
For those travelling by car, the
A83 has regular roadworks and
convoys due to landslides, while
on a summer weekend the road
along Loch Lomond is often
stop-start.

The route

⑤ Start with a gentle gravel climb out of the car park and past
the forest gates. You get glimpses of views over the waters of
the famous Loch Long in the areas of clear felling. The climb
flattens out then the track becomes more undulating, with a
few turns off the main track to avoid.

② You soon reach a signpost for *The Dukes Path* at the small
Corran Lochan. This is where the fun begins. A mostly rideable singletrack climb takes you alongside the lochan before
a steeper section in the trees marks the end of the climb.

③ From here you need to be on your top gravel game – it is 4km
of steep, loose singletrack, but then it's smooth and fun, before
another steep, loose surprise. If you have false teeth, they'll
soon be rattled out.

④ Finally, after a couple of steep sections, you'll be back on the
forest road. While experienced riders will clean the lot on drop
bars, most mere mortals will be off the bike a couple of times at
least on the steeper sections. The track soon takes your breath
away for other reasons as you see the view of Lochgoilhead and
the craggy peaks behind it.

1 THE RELIEF OF A SMOOTH TRACK NEAR LOCHGOILHEAD. 2 WHAT TO EXPECT ON THE DUKES PATH SINGLETRACK.

5 After a farm gate with an old sign warning about angry live-stock, you join a tarmac road past some houses before it merges with a narrow back road. Regain your breath as the climbing begins again soon, and it goes on for a while.

6 Take the next right-hand turn on to a gravel track. This track reaches an altitude of over 300m at the head of Glen Croe with its famous Rest and be Thankful stone. You stay on the opposite side of the glen and enjoy a flat-out, fast descent.

7 As you start to climb again the track ends and a path starts. The OS map does actually mark this if you look closely. The path crosses a kind of rocky gorge using a bridge; once over the bridge, a short techy hairpin path takes you back to another track. You now have a fast, smooth descent back to the car park where you started.

Other routes or attractions in the area

The best and easiest gravel add-on is to detour into Lochgoilhead village and then on to gravel tracks on the opposite side of Loch Goil. Take the track past Lettermay and on to some new forest tracks that take you north to where the B828 joins the B839. Here you can rejoin the rest of the route after adding in about 10 kilometres of primo gravel.

If you want to avoid the short, technical singletrack section above Glen Croe you can take a left-hand fork to descend towards the A83 and, just before the main road, follow a track to Ardgartan and rejoin the route to finish.

For a weekender linear ride, why not combine with **09 Loch Eck and Loch Long** (pages 77–83) and then catch the ferry back to the 'mainland' station at Gourock, west of Glasgow.

11 CRINAN, LOCH SWEEN AND FAERY ISLES VIEWS
49KM/30 MILES

Introduction

This loop is true west coast riding and one of the least technical routes in the book. However, at 49 kilometres and with over 500 metres of ascent, it shouldn't be taken too lightly. The hilly coastal section provides great views out towards the Paps of Jura; the views over the Faery Isles and Loch Sween are also excellent. Other than a few steeper inclines it is never too challenging; it is a thoroughly pleasant day out.

The local area

Crinan is a picture postcard little fishing harbour where the Crinan Canal ends after linking Loch Crinan to Lochgilphead. This short canal was planned by James Watt and finished in 1809; it lets ships avoid the long detour around the Mull of Kintyre. This gravel route uses a dramatic section of the towpath back into Crinan, where the canal hugs the coastline and there's a drop down to a beach from the towpath. There is a quaint little lighthouse at Crinan, where the final canal lock exits into the sea; this area is a popular photo stop too.

The route highlight is the gravel riding along Loch Sween and the views it offers to the Faery Isles. It turns out there's probably no fairies on these uninhabited wooded islands, although few people ever visit the islands to verify. It seems unclear how the islands got their name, most likely from the wild mythical feel of the islands' isolated Celtic rainforest.

As you ride around the coast it is mostly plantation forest but there are pockets of ancient weather-beaten oak forest

OPPOSITE ONE OF THE MANY GREAT VIEWS OVER LOCH CRINAN TO DUNTRUNE CASTLE.

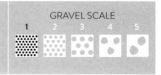

DISTANCE **49km/30 miles** — ASCENT **556m/1,824ft** — OFF-ROAD **40%**
START/FINISH **Crinan** — START/FINISH GRID REF **NR 788943**
SATNAV **PA31 8SR** — GPS **56.0901, -5.5573** — MAP **Landranger 55, Lochgilphead & Loch Awe (1:50,000)**

GRAVEL SCALE

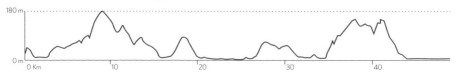

GRAVEL RIDES SCOTLAND

thick with moss and lichen on the trees, which probably says more about the weather than you want to know. The area has also now had beavers reintroduced, making it even wetter in places; there is an informative visitor centre at Barnluasgan with walkways to see the beaver dams – the animals themselves are harder to see.

Route overview

The route is a figure of eight starting in the picturesque village of Crinan. Starting here means a nice steady climb to warm up along the road and a final warm down riding back along the canal towpath.

The gravel riding is never technical, but it is one of those routes that undulates enough to leave you deceptively knackered without blaming any climb. Either of the loops can be tackled on their own, so if 49 kilometres sounds too much, pick your half.

If riding on a hot day, factor in time for a swim at Carsaig Bay, where the first section of gravel joins the road. The eastern part of the route is away from the coast but offers equally fun gravel riding through rich forests and past small lochans along the way.

Navigation

Navigation is relatively straight-forward with large sections on roads. Be aware that there are cycling routes marked on OS maps, but these aren't signposted on the ground.

If you ride this route anti-clockwise that means you ride the coastal section first and can decide in the middle whether to return to the pub or set off on the second loop and *really* earn those chips and beer.

Facilities and refreshments

Crinan is a popular tourist stop and has a good cafe, pub and restaurants, all connected to the **Crinan Hotel**. The hotel pub has a fun, cosy nautical theme and, with a warming fire, is perfect for a post-ride stop on a wild weather day. There's a good selection of whisky too.

Tayvallich has a cafe, pub and a basic but useful general store.

OPPOSITE THE PHOTOGENIC MINI LIGHTHOUSE AT CRINAN NEAR THE CANAL SEA LOCK.

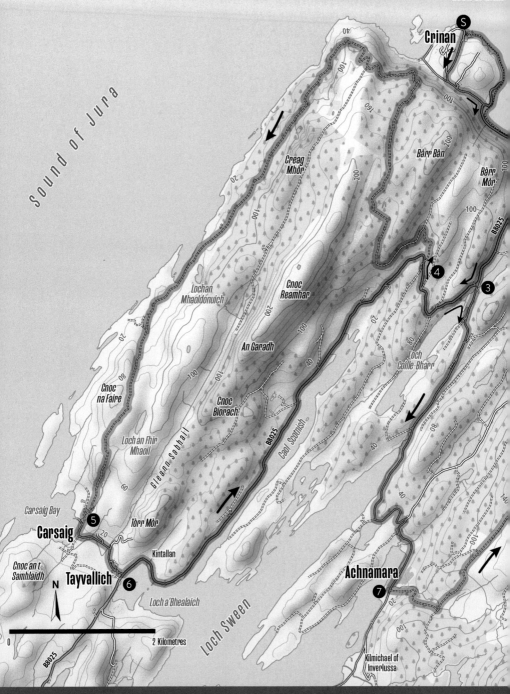

Loch Crinan

Crinan **S**

Sound of Jura

Bàrr Bàn

Creag Mhòr

Bàrr Mòr

B8025

4

Cnoc Reamhar

3

Lochan Mhaoldònuich

Loch Coille-Bharr

An Garadh

Cnoc na Faire

Cnoc Biorach

Caol Scotnish

Gleann Sabhail

B8025

Loch an Fhir Mhaoil

Carsaig Bay

Tòrr Mòr

5

Carsaig

Kintallan

Achnamara

Cnoc an t-Samhlaidh

Tayvallich **6**

7

N

Loch a'Bhealaich

Loch Sween

0   2 Kilometres

B8025

Kilmichael of Inverlussa

GRAVEL RIDES SCOTLAND

The route

S Start from Crinan and head back out along the B841, the only road out of the village. Don't follow the canal towpath as there is no bridge for a while and you'll be on the wrong side of the canal for the first loop.

2 Take the first right turn to start climbing; it's a steady climb, but nothing too hard.

3 You'll pass signs to a beaver reintroduction visitor centre as the road flattens at Barnluasgan. Follow the road uphill for a mellow 1.5 kilometres until you reach the third forest gravel track on the right.

4 Turn right on to this track. Keep following this gravel track as it undulates with epic sea views between faster plantation sections.

5 A fun descent zigzags down to Carsaig and a lovely shallow sandy bay.

6 Back on the road you'll pass the cafe, pub and general store at Tayvallich. Follow the road past Caol Scotnish to return to Barnluasgan. Turn right here to start the second loop (or continue straight ahead to return to Crinan).

7 At the far end of the village of Achnamara, turn left on to a gravel track, leaving the road behind. The climb quickly leaves sea level behind to reach a height of over 150m.

8 The gravel track follows the forest edge, past lochans and some nice views. A few junctions will need careful navigation. Return to the road and turn left.

9 Turn right to cross the canal. Turn left to follow the towpath, which is also Sustrans National Route 78, all the way back into Crinan.

Bike shops
There are no bike shops in the local area.

Public transport and access
There are no public transport links in the local area.

There are car parks at both ends of Crinan. These are clearly signposted, but they do get busy in peak summer season so arrive early if you can.

Other routes or attractions in the area
The best add-on is an out-and-back to Taynish National Nature Reserve near Tayvallich, but look at the map and you'll find a maze of rideable tracks further east and south to detour on to. The best option for a weekend bikepacking trip is to follow the coast south-west from Achnamara to Kilmory. From here head back north and pick up Sustrans National Route 78 to reach Lochgilphead and then follow the Crinan Canal back to Crinan. An easy but rewarding weekend adventure.

OPPOSITE RIDING THE COASTAL TRACK LOOKING OUT TOWARDS THE FAERY ISLES.

12 AN SUIDHE WIND FARM AND EREDINE FOREST

32KM/20 MILES

Introduction

A short but very sweet ride which makes a great little adventure up and around some elevated wind farm tracks, offering epic views of the Arrochar Alps, Loch Awe, Loch Fyne and even further afield.

The local area

There is so much good gravel riding around the Loch Awe area that it was hard to select this route. This one has exceptional views and is certainly a bit more varied than a route in the slightly monotonous but vast network of plantation forest tracks to the north of Loch Awe would be.

The start of this route is near the Auchindrain Township – a collection of traditional Highland longhouse buildings and a visitor centre. They recommend 60–90 minutes to explore the site, which is a genuine piece of history as well as an open-air museum. It has chickens and livestock wandering about too. If you're powering out the miles, you can probably leave your family here to enjoy themselves while you complete the route.

Just down the road is Inveraray, the black and white town. In this planned Victorian new town all the shops are strictly painted black and white, even the well-known shop logos which are usually coloured. It is one of the best examples of an eighteenth-century new town in Scotland, all created by the Dukes of Argyll, with a woollen mill, workers' cottages, inns, a church and a pier for herring fishing. It normally has a queue for ice creams, and it has a good fish and chip shop too.

OPPOSITE A FAST BUT WELL-USED GRAVEL SECTION NEAR THE START OF THE RIDE.

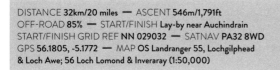

DISTANCE **32km/20 miles** — ASCENT **546m/1,791ft**
OFF-ROAD **85%** — START/FINISH **Lay-by near Auchindrain**
START/FINISH GRID REF **NN 029032** — SATNAV **PA32 8WD**
GPS **56.1805, -5.1772** — MAP **OS Landranger 55, Lochgilphead & Loch Awe; 56 Loch Lomond & Inveraray (1:50,000)**

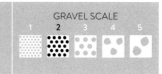

GRAVEL SCALE
1 2 3 4 5

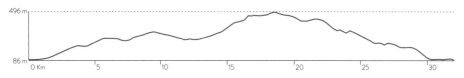

GRAVEL RIDES SCOTLAND

With all this local history in evidence, the modern industrial development of wind turbines and associated new pylons along the route itself becomes even starker. Combined with significant recent forest felling it can feel a little less wild than some other areas of Scotland; however, these developments are why the tracks exist and it is a great wee ride to the top of a hill looking out across a wild area.

Route overview

This ride has a big climb on good gravel, before riding a loop of an exposed, but scenic, wind farm. The descent is on marginally rougher tracks. It has a gravel rating of 2 out of 5, as some gravel is coarse but the tracks are generally well surfaced with no real surprises. The tracks can have pick-up trucks driving on them; be particularly aware of this when descending.

Once you clear the treeline you can enjoy panoramic views of the surrounding mountains and lochs; Loch Fyne is to the south while Loch Awe is to the north. There is an easy add-on option to extend the route to Loch Awe, and a longer add-on to the shoreline of Loch Fyne is fun and pretty straightforward.

Navigation

The route is probably best ridden clockwise as the short road section on the A83 is mostly downhill and therefore faster. The A83 is quite a fast road and at peak times is busy, so be careful and stay visible. In either direction, the climb to the top is long and tough.

While researching the route in 2021 there were new tracks being built around a substation and pylons near the start, so be aware that these might not be on your map yet when navigating.

Facilities and refreshments

Auchindrain Township has a cafe with basic food and drink; opening hours vary so check before you visit. There are no other facilities on the route. There is a good selection of cafes, pubs and shops in Inveraray (on the A83 north of the route), and a well-stocked village shop in Furnace (on the A83 south of the route).

OPPOSITE FORCED TO STOP AND TAKE IN THE VIEW WHEN DESCENDING FROM THE WIND FARM.

12 **AN SUIDHE WIND FARM AND EREDINE FOREST**

103

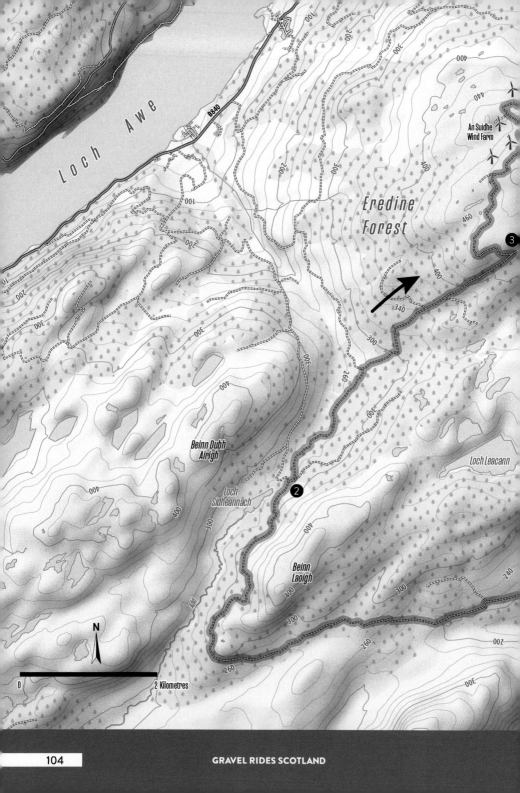

Loch Awe

B840

Eredine
Forest

An Suidhe
Wind Farm

③

Beinn Dubh
Airigh

Loch
Sidheannach

Loch Leacann

②

Beinn
Laoigh

N

0   2 Kilometres

GRAVEL RIDES SCOTLAND

GRAVEL RIDES SCOTLAND

LOOKING OUT AT ANOTHER NEW WIND FARM IN THE DISTANCE.

The route

S The route starts at Auchindrain on a narrow tarmac dead-end road – head west on this road. This soon fades into good quality gravel. The initial gravel track passes by new pylons and pylon tracks. This carries on into the forest. Don't forget to look behind to see the views. Once in the forest, it is a steady climb uphill – those views don't come easy!

2 About 11km in to the route, just after Loch Sidheannach, there is a track on the left heading down to Loch Awe and then, a little further along, another track back up from Loch Awe meets our route – this makes a nice detour to make our route longer and mix things up. Keep straight ahead to follow our route.

3 An Suidhe Wind Farm soon appears – turn left to start a scenic loop of the site. It is a great spot with panoramic views and nice wee lochans, albeit slightly overshadowed by the 24 turbines.

4 The descent has more distracting mountain views but is fast and feels deceptively long. It is a blast. Cross over the bridge and keep on the higher track above the river.

5 You are soon back on the road and hopefully refreshed enough to get this section out the way quickly. The A83 can feel quite busy but there is good visibility on this 2km section back to where you started.

Bike shops
Campbell Bike Workshop
(T: 07811 123 943) is based at Mansefield Studios in Arrochar village.

Public transport and access
There are no train stations or bike-friendly buses within a practical distance.

There are parking lay-bys on the A83 near Auchindrain, or if you visit Auchindrain Township you can ask about parking there.

Other routes or attractions in the area
The obvious add-on is taking a left turn down to Loch Awe mid route, either for a long loop of the loch for multi-day riding or simply turning back uphill again on the next gravel track. In the other direction there are great gravel tracks along Loch Fyne past Furnace; head north-east along coastal gravel to Rubha nam Frangach, then head west to Calonairigh and rejoin our route on the A83.

OPPOSITE ENJOYING THE VIEW AND NEW GRAVEL TRACK AT THE WIND FARM.

SWEEPING VIEWS OF LOCH ARD
NEAR ABERFOYLE (ROUTE 13).

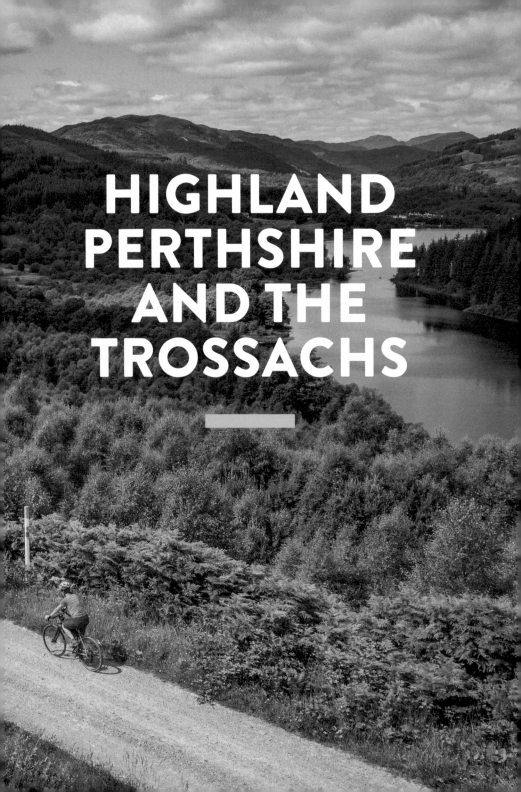

HIGHLAND PERTHSHIRE AND THE TROSSACHS

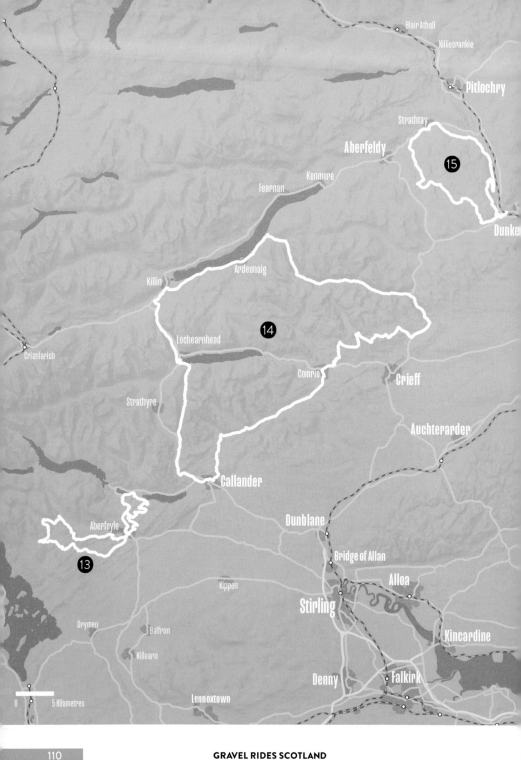

Blair Atholl

Killiecrankie

Pitlochry

Strathtay

Aberfeldy

⑮

Kenmore

Fearnan

Dunke

Ardeonaig

Killin

⑭

Lochearnhead

Crianlarich

Comrie

Crieff

Strathyre

Auchterarder

Callander

Aberfoyle

Dunblane

⑬

Bridge of Allan

Alloa

Kippen

Stirling

Kincardine

Drymen

Balfron

Killearn

Denny **Falkirk**

Lennoxtown

0   5 Kilometres

HIGHLAND PERTHSHIRE AND THE TROSSACHS

Highland Perthshire and the Trossachs are both very popular gravel destinations. This is the heart of Scotland where the Highlands, defined as the area to the north of the Highland Boundary Fault line, really start to rise up. This geology delivers long finger-shaped lochs, natural forests and craggy peaks, all contained by the iconic Loch Lomond in the west. To prove that this is a real fault line, the town of Comrie is sometimes referred to as the 'Shaky Toun' – it is said that during the 1830s over 7,000 earth tremors were recorded in the area.

Much of this area is within the Loch Lomond and the Trossachs National Park – an area always popular with hikers, bikers and visitors alike. The area is criss-crossed with ancient drove roads, military roads, forest tracks and wind farms, making it a gravelleur's dream. The routes included here barely scratch the surface, but they showcase the customarily smooth gravel tracks. It's a great place to dip your toes into Scottish gravel for those getting started.

Such is the volume of gravel riding that two areas have pitched themselves as gravel capitals – Aberfoyle, aka Gravelfoyle, and Perthshire Gravel. More information about existing and planned waymarked routes is available online.

Be aware that wild camping close to many of the accessible lochs is banned in the national park between March and September. Aimed at so-called dirty campers, it doesn't really affect bikepacking and camping in the middle of nowhere, but it is enforced and worth remembering when planning trips. It is also a useful reminder of the privilege of wild camping and ensuring you leave no trace – as wild camping should be done.

13 ABERFOYLE AKA GRAVELFOYLE – NORTH AND SOUTH LOOPS
60KM/37 MILES

Introduction

Aberfoyle is probably the closest Scotland gets to the classic gravel grinding miles of North America. The tracks are remarkably smooth and well maintained across the area, the views are epic and the options are endless. It's perfect for all riders and even for taking kids in seats or trailers. The route also easily splits into two or three shorter loops.

The local area

Aberfoyle is a great place to start and in the large central car park you'll notice other gravel bikes being unloaded. Nowhere else has set out their stall quite like 'Gravelfoyle' for attracting gravelistas to the outstanding local riding.

The area has long been known as having a few mountain bike trails in the forests but who knew it was the endless tracks in between that would turn out to be the area's crowning jewel? The forest roads are for some unknown reason smoother and better maintained than almost anywhere else in Scotland.

Aberfoyle itself is a classic Scottish tourist town with souvenir shops and tour buses parked up and even a wool centre with sheep grazing at its heart. The high street has a good selection of food and drink offerings. Its location on the river gives the town a pleasant feel. The concept of Gravelfoyle as a destination arose from the Dukes Weekender, a gravel event that follows a similar route to our ride.

The most iconic feature seen on the ride is the water pipeline stretching from Loch Katrine to Mugdock Reservoir, which supports

OPPOSITE THE INFAMOUS GRAVELFOYLE AQUEDUCT.

DISTANCE **60km/37 miles** — ASCENT **917m/3,009ft** — OFF-ROAD **65%**
START/FINISH **Aberfoyle** — START/FINISH GRID REF **NN 520010**
SATNAV **FK8 3SZ** — GPS **56.1786, -4.3858** — MAP **OS Landranger 56,**
Loch Lomond & Inveraray; 57, Stirling & the Trossachs (1:50,000)

GRAVEL SCALE

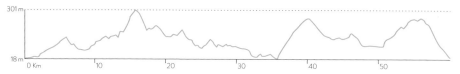

1 LATE SUMMER MEANS BLAEBERRY SEASON. **2** THE PRISTINE ABERFOYLE TRACKS ARE SMOOTH ENOUGH FOR CHILD TRAILERS.

Navigation

Navigating is helped on some of the route by frequent signs back to Aberfoyle, but it is mostly plantation forest and there are a lot of junctions to navigate so be prepared. The Gravelfoyle project intends to waymark some gravel routes here too as soon as allowed. The northern loop is much easier to navigate as you mostly follow the road and then the forest drive, but the climb up Duke's Pass isn't easy.

Glasgow's water supply. It is an impressive Victorian feat of engineering which was overseen by John Bateman and completed in 1859; it involved raising the water level of Loch Katrine by 1.2 metres and the construction of 42 kilometres of aqueducts and 21 kilometres of tunnels through hard rock. There are a number of tunnel ventilation shafts along the route. These round towers, with hoops of metal over the top, pop up in the middle of nowhere and you'll wonder what they are for. All in, the scheme is said to have cost £2.3 billion in today's money and it is still supplying Glasgow today, with relatively few modernisations.

Route overview

The route can easily be split into two loops – the Duke's Pass and Three Lochs Forest Drive to the north, and a southern loop ending alongside Loch Ard. The only section of the whole route which is vaguely technical is the final path descent into Aberfoyle from the north, even though this is still a relatively-well-surfaced path.

This area and Aberfoyle itself are perfect for families; if taking a trailer or child seat, the smooth gravel and gentle undulations on the first half of the southern loop works best. The Duke's Pass involves a tough climb up from Aberfoyle so it's best to leave the children behind for this bit.

THE LARGE TREES AND SWEEPING LANDSCAPE BESIDE LOCH ARD MAKES YOU FEEL SMALL HERE.

The southern loop is pretty much forest bound on good tracks for the first 15 kilometres, but takes in a couple of the interesting pipeline aqueducts. The route avoids the first bridge over Duchray Water at Duchray Cottage, because it has locked gates; there is a stile, but if you have a kids' trailer or any mobility issues it isn't feasible, so the route avoids this.

The climb to Duke's Pass is steep and the Three Lochs Forest Drive is open to cars (a fee is payable for cars; bikes can travel for free) and can get busy although it is all relative; drivers tend to go slow as driving on gravel appears to be a novelty for most.

Lochside camping is restricted in the Loch Lomond and the Trossachs National Park; most of the route passes through this Camping Management Zone, which applies between March and September. The Three Lochs Forest Drive and one end of Loch Ard have some lovely camping spots that can be booked. The fine for camping without a permit is up to £500. However, away from the lochside areas, wild camping is not restricted. While it may not seem enforceable in the middle of nowhere, police vehicles have been seen on the gravel roads in the camping areas so do plan ahead.

www.lochlomond-trossachs.org/things-to-do/camping/go-wild

Facilities and refreshments
Aberfoyle has several cafes and useful shops; the popular **Aberfoyle Delicatessen** often has a queue outside for its quality pies and there is a small supermarket for overnight provisions.

The Scottish Wool Centre in Aberfoyle has rare breed sheep, a cafe and sheepdog displays in peak season.

B829

Loch Chon

Beinn Bhreac

Beinn Dubh

Ledard Glen

Gleann Dubh

Loch Dubh

Duchray Water

Stob a' Bhlair Bhain

Water of Chon

Kinlochard

B829

Loch Ard

Tom Dubh nan Caorach

Meall Dubh

Bad Dearg

Bruach Caorainn Burn

3

340

Druim nam Mial

4

Barr a Ghartain

Innis Ard

2

Beinn Uird

N

Gleann Meadhonach

Queen Elizabeth Forest Park

0   2 Kilometres

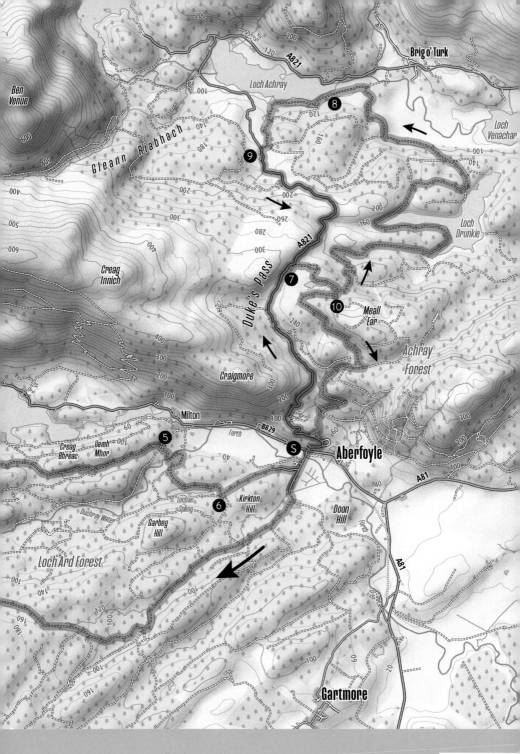

THE LOCHAN SPLING FISH SCULPTURE IS WORTH A STOP.

Bike shops

Aberfoyle Bike Hire & Cafe (T: 01877 382 023) is in the centre of town, with spares and repairs.

Public transport and access

The nearest train station to the route is at Dunblane, about 25 kilometres from the northern loop.

Parking is free in the central car park in Aberfoyle; there is usually ample space.

The route

S Starting from the centre of Aberfoyle, head over the old bridge on the River Forth and follow the dead end road until it turns to gravel. It has a no entry sign for vehicles but continue riding. The first section is all through forest with few reference points so it needs some careful navigation to stay on the right track. It undulates up and down and after about 3km you get the first dramatic view of the peak of Ben Lomond ahead.

2 Continue on until you reach a signpost for *Duchray Cottage*. (This track cuts the southern loop in half but takes you to a bridge with locked gates. There are stiles but with ebikes or for a less able rider it is worth remembering.) Keep left at this signpost to carry on along the main track on the full loop. This is where the hills get bigger and the views better. At the time of writing a lot of tree harvesting had been ongoing, helping to open up views, but also meaning that some new tracks are rougher or might not be on your map yet. Keep heading uphill admiring views of Ben Lomond. Three switchbacks tell you the top is close.

3 Cross the burn. The descent is steep but keeps flowing until the bridge over the Duchray Water; cross the bridge then turn right and follow the track. At the next junction both tracks lead to Loch Ard; turn left to follow our route.

4 As you approach Loch Ard, turn right on to a high track which offers stunning views; alternatively you can follow the lochside track which is a bit rougher.

GRAVEL RIDES SCOTLAND

A LOCKED GATE NEAR DUCHRAY COTTAGE MEANS A DETOUR.

5 You next reach Loch Ard Forest car park – firstly an overflow one and then the main car park. On the right is a green marker post for a path; follow this path across a pedestrian bridge over Duchray Water. Keep left and at Lochan Spling watch out for a wooden fish sculpture in the water.

6 Keep left again to join a back road then turn left to reach the old bridge over the River Forth where you started. You can call it a day here or take a cafe stop in Aberfoyle and then head on to the A821 up the Duke's Pass for the northern loop. This side of the pass is quite steep.

7 Once you reach the top you will see the *Three Lochs Forest Drive* clearly signposted; turn right on to the forest drive. Along the forest drive you pass Lochan Reòidhte and Loch Drunkie. The forest drive is waymarked; our route follows a traffic-free detour before Loch Drunkie.

8 Pass along the southern shore of Loch Achray then reach the A821 again.

9 Turn left along the A821 and climb back up to the top of the Duke's Pass on a mellower gradient. Once at the top, turn left on to the Three Lochs Forest Drive again.

10 This time turn right on to a track with a barrier across following the signpost for *National Cycle Route 7*. Follow the Sustrans National Route 7 down into Aberfoyle; it is mostly a track with one well-surfaced path section near the end.

Other routes or attractions in the area
There are just too many to include for day ride options; Gravelfoyle is worth checking out for some ideas **www.facebook. com/Gravelfoyle** This ride can also be combined with **14 Callander and Loch Tay monster loop** (pages 121–127) for a bikepacking trip.

14 CALLANDER AND LOCH TAY MONSTER LOOP
128KM/80 MILES

Introduction

The name doesn't mislead; this is a proper monster of a ride. It can be approached as either an epic single-day ride or split into two for a bikepacking overnighter. It really has everything that makes Scottish gravel riding great. It is rated 2 out of 5 as it is mostly on smooth tracks or tarmac back roads, but there are some short challenges along the way.

The local area

This area has an infinite amount of outstanding gravel riding, and it was too hard to leave anything out, so this route kept getting longer and longer until a monster was born. While it is long, it is also designed to be easily cut down into two shorter routes. The complete ride is a full taster menu of Scottish gravel: it has classic military roads, drove roads, dramatic hill tracks, towering avenues of fir trees and cycle paths over magical Harry-Potter-esque viaducts.

The ride starts in Callander, a popular tourist town that can be busy in summer, but it is hard to believe how quickly a gravel bike lets you leave almost every other person behind. Saying that, the climb from Callander is steep and certainly not quick.

The ride also passes through the picturesque towns of Comrie, Killin and Lochearnhead. Killin, in particular, is in a great location with the Falls of Dochart cascading through the centre of the town as the road bridge spans across. North of the bridge, down a flight of steps and under an arch, is the Clan MacNab Burial Ground on an island in the river. The gate is locked but you can request access locally.

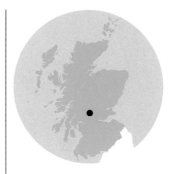

OPPOSITE THE EPIC GRAVEL TRACK LEADING NORTH FROM CALLANDER.

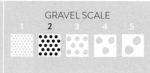

DISTANCE **128km/80 miles** — ASCENT **1,667m/5,469ft** — OFF-ROAD **60%**
START/FINISH **Callander** — START/FINISH GRID REF **NN 627080**
SATNAV **FK17 8AN** — GPS **56.2446, -4.2172** — MAP OS Landranger 51, Loch Tay & Glen Dochart; 52, Pitlochry & Crieff; 57, Stirling & the Trossachs; 58, Perth & Alloa (1:50,000)

GRAVEL SCALE

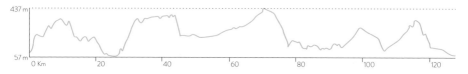

THE IMPOSING LOCH TURRET RESERVOIR.

Navigation

The route is written in an anticlockwise direction. This gives better options to cut the route short along Loch Earn and also means more fast, long descents and shorter, steeper slogs uphill. This is a long, remote and wild trail so clear navigation is vital; you can quickly end up a long way off course in the hills here. From Loch Tay, you can follow Sustrans National Route 7 to get back to the start.

Facilities and refreshments

If you take two days and don't rush through this ride you can enjoy stopping for good food and coffee in the popular hot spots of Callander, Comrie, Killin and Lochearnhead. All have good cafes, pubs and fish and chips too. Callander is the largest town on the route and makes a great place to start the ride and

There is a section of cycle path near Lochearnhead that often floods because of the beavers that have been reintroduced to the area. The little munchers might not be seen but you can't miss their dam as it is big enough to flood the path up to your pedals.

The route follows sections of old military roads, the highlight being a section of General Wade's route from Creiff north to Dalnacardoch which was built in 1730. Just before Comrie is Cultybraggan Camp, an old prisoner of war camp which is now a fascinating museum with most buildings retained; bizarrely, it is also a municipal recycling centre.

Comrie is a nice little town and is home to the historic Earthquake House, a listed seismic measuring station built in 1874. Near Comrie is the base of Comrie Croft, a locally-owned mountain bike trail centre with a cafe and some cool accommodation. It's worth a stop even if the main trails are too techy for gravel bikes.

Route overview

This loop can be a midsummer single-day ride to test the fittest or, more realistically, a fun weekend bikepacking ride. If you choose the latter, then an overnight stop to wild camp responsibly in Glen Almond splits the route well.

The mix of classic Scottish hill tracks, Sustrans off-road cycle paths and quiet singletrack roads means that it is suited to a wide

1 SUPERB GRAVEL IN GLEN ALMOND. **2** GOOD TRACKS JUST BEFORE THE SHORT BOGGY HIKE-A-BIKE SECTION IN GLEN ALMOND.

range of riders, however long they take to cover the distance. There are obvious options to make two separate loops by using the fun road on the southern shore of Loch Earn. This area of Scotland is a great place to base yourself for multiple days of proper gravel adventures.

What makes this area and ride special is that the long, remote gravel tracks are out on the open fells and away from plantation forests. These are a long way from any roads or towns and, while they are not perfect gravel, they are still firmly rideable by gravel bike. As with most upland tracks, some sections get steep and loose, such as the top of the climb after Comrie, while others are on weathered, rough gravel, like the fun but steep descent to the A822 before Glen Almond. There is one section of boggy path towards the head of Glen Almond where, realistically, all riders will be on and off the bike. It is clearly marked as a path rather than a track on OS maps. This section is short lived; you soon reach another track at a building called Dunan on OS maps. Glen Ample has some burn crossings and the weathered grass-down-the-middle track can feel even rougher than it should do as you are towards the end of a long ride; you may opt to stay on the easier cycle path instead.

The long watery fingers of Loch Earn and Loch Tay both have similar lochside single-track roads on their southern shores; both are perfect for a gravel bike with so many ups and downs and even some loose, banked corners.

finish with some good food or a stop at the small supermarket for supplies.

Comrie Croft is just outside Comrie and has accommodation options including katas, or teepees, and a very good cafe. Most of the food is grown next to the car park on-site and there's a farm shop too.

Bike shops

Wheels Cycling Centre (T: 01877 331 100) is on the south side of Callander near Loch Venachar. Focused on hire bikes, it also offers servicing; it is open reduced hours or appointment only during the shoulder season. Along the route, **Comrie Croft Bikes** (T: 01764 670 140) is a great little bike shop; they are located to the east of Comrie with repairs and spares.

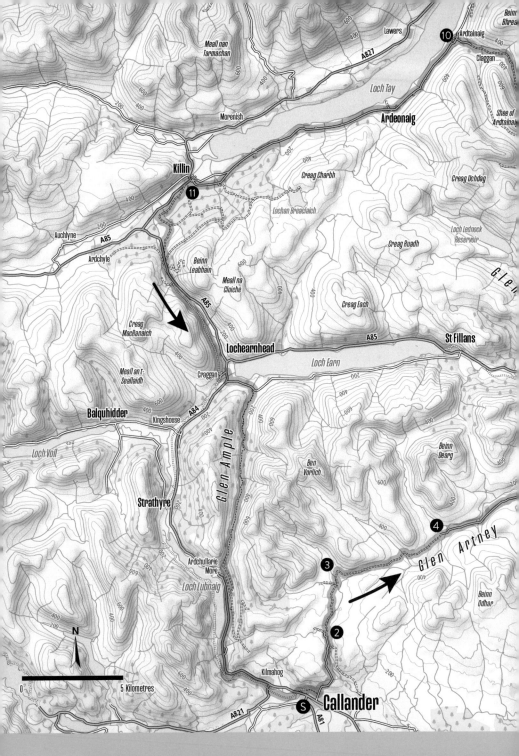

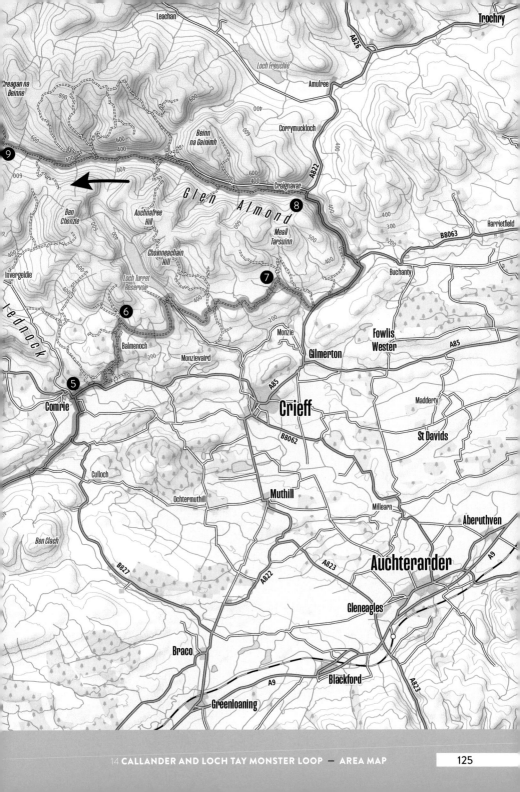

THE LONG AND FUN DESCENT TOWARDS LOCH TAY.

There are train stations at
Dunblane, Perth and Dunkeld,
all about 20 kilometres away
from the route. The logical
option is to start at Dunkeld
railway station and combine
this ride with **15 Dunkeld and
the Tay Forest Park** (pages
129–135), connecting through
Aberfeldy.

There are several car parks
in Callander, mainly pay and
display.

For more challenging gravel
you can detour south-west from
Killin along Glen Dochart. To
make the route shorter, simply
head west from Comrie and
head along the southern shore
of Loch Earn; at the western
end of the loch join Sustrans
National Route 7 to return to
Callander.

To make the route even
longer you can head south-west
from Callander and ride over to
Aberfoyle on good gravel tracks
and quiet roads. You could make
this into a linear ride using
Balloch railway station, which is
the nearest station to Aberfoyle.

The route

S From Callander follow a steep single-track road climb heading
north. The road gets steeper and steeper before levelling out
with fantastic views over your shoulder towards the Lowlands
around Stirling. Up ahead, the mountains loom large, and the
gravel track leads straight towards them.

2 The gravel track starts with some ups and downs and the views
get better and better with each small summit.

3 Two buildings appear and these signal the time to turn right.
They look like bothies but they are locked estate buildings. The
track carries on as perfect gravel through this classic Trossachs
upland landscape. Take time to absorb the surroundings as gravel
riding doesn't get much better than this.

4 Finally, a bumpy descent spits you out on a rollercoaster singletrack road alongside the Water of Ruchill. Despite many small
ups and downs it's mostly downhill to Comrie. On the way
you'll pass Cultybraggan (if doing a shorter loop you can cut
back on gravel to the south side of Loch Earn past St Fillans
from here).

5 Comrie has a few places to grab food and a fish and chip shop,
but it's a small place. The next section can be hard to navigate
as you skirt around West Lodge Caravan Park and through
the grounds of a large private house and head towards Comrie
Croft. Behind Comrie Croft the track climbs with a few hairpins;
it is all at a good grade and rideable. The track finally breaks
clear of the trees and offers great panoramic views.

6 This next section feels a bit like the Yorkshire Dales as a rockier
gravel track heads to Loch Turret Reservoir. The track carries

A ROMANTICALLY LOCATED ESTATE BUILDING (UNFORTUNATELY NOT A BOTHY) ALONG GLEN ARTNEY.

on south and has a few steep-sided burns to cross which appear quite suddenly – you will need to be on your toes if you're tired or it's getting late.

7 Turn right and a delightful, long gravel descent takes you down to the A822. Turn left on to the A822; it is not a particularly busy road, but it is an A road and the cars can be fast so make sure you have good lights and visibility if it is gloomy. This road section will fly by as it is mostly downhill so quickly eats into the miles as a reprieve before more gravel goodness.

8 The bridge over the River Almond signals a left turn on to excellent gravel estate tracks. As you get higher up into Glen Almond there are some good wild camping spots for those taking their time over the route. All good things must come to an end and the gravel turns to mud 2km after Dalriech, a lone estate cottage (again there are no bothies here). The grass track along Glen Almond can be hard work and there are some sections on and off the bike. It is usually very wet, but in summer or dry spells it is generally fine.

9 At Dunan, a new hydro track goes off uphill to the left – this is possibly not on your map but ignore it and head north towards Loch Tay on yet another epic, long gravel descent.

10 Loch Tay's southern shore has another classic lochside rollercoaster road that might not be gravel but is just as fun. It will sap your energy though. (The Rob Roy Way heads south from Loch Tay; don't be tempted to follow it because this 3km section becomes a very muddy hike-a-bike.)

11 At Killin, admire the stunning Falls of Dochart and grab a coffee in one of the two hotels near the bridge. There's a small shop selling basic supplies too. Now you have a choice; either follow the signposted Sustrans National Route 7, which is the quickest and easiest way back to Callander (34km), or follow our slightly longer (35km) route. It starts on Sustrans National Route 7 (remember to take a bell!), goes across the engineers' delight of Glen Ogle Viaduct and then leaves Sustrans National Route 7 at Lochearnhead and takes a track into Glen Ample. This is slow going in places, but it is scenic, wild and normally all gravel-bike-friendly. There are a few burns to cross so watch out in wet weather. There is then a section on the main road before you can rejoin Sustrans National Route 7 back into Callander to complete the route.

15 DUNKELD AND THE TAY FOREST PARK
51KM/32 MILES

Introduction

This route has a good mix of road and tracks through dark forests and open farmland; the highlight is the epic view when you ride through a wind farm.

The local area

Dunkeld really feels like the start of the Highlands as you head north along the A9. It sits on the River Tay and is fast becoming a hub for all kinds of cycling. From gravel riding to road and even full-on downhill mountain biking, this area has it all within the surrounding forests and hills. The historic town itself has gone from strength to strength with an abundance of accommodation and places get good food and coffee. Within the town is a well-preserved historic centre including Dunkeld Cathedral which lost its roof during the Reformation in the 1560s. Nearby is Birnam and its famous oak tree which was referenced in Shakespeare's *Macbeth*.

The Hermitage, where the ride starts, is a fascinating place; huge Douglas fir trees tower over the paths leading to the Black Linn Falls, where the River Braan crashes down into the deep pools below, all visible as you stand on the stone Hermitage Bridge which arches above. The whole scene is covered in green moss and it looks very natural, but it is part of wider designed grounds and is loaded with history. The buildings, including Hermitage Bridge and Ossian's Hall, were built by the Dukes of Atholl and add intrigue to the site.

Further into the route at Grandtully you'll find Iain Burnett's chocolate shop and cafe; it feels a bit posh for muddy bikers, but

OPPOSITE THE GREEN, MOSSY WOODLAND AT THE HERMITAGE NEAR DUNKELD.

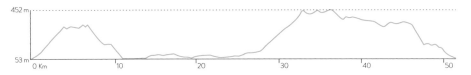

DISTANCE **51km/32 miles** — ASCENT **810m/2,657ft**
OFF-ROAD **65%** — START/FINISH **The Hermitage, west of Dunkeld**
START/FINISH GRID REF **NO 013422** — SATNAV **PH8 0JR**
GPS **56.5614, -3.6075** — MAP **OS Landranger 52, Pitlochry & Crieff (1:50,000)**

GRAVEL SCALE
1 2 3 4 5

GRAVEL RIDES SCOTLAND

it is so loaded with chocolates you might just blend in on a muddy day. This small village has a nice campsite and pub too.

Above Grandtully, the route heads around a large wind farm to the north-west of Dunkeld; this neighbours another large wind farm nearer Aberfeldy – they both offer many tracks and riding options. However, the natural beauty has undoubtedly been shattered with so many turbines. Aberfeldy is a pretty town just off the route, but it is surrounded by gravel tracks and this route could easily be extended towards Aberfeldy.

Route overview

The route is on mostly good tracks with a long road stint near the start. The atmospheric towering forest around The Hermitage has enough options to ride that you can stay here all day going around in circles. For those with half an eye on more technical riding, the forest is scattered with enduro mountain bike trails and was a popular stop on the Scottish Enduro Series MTB race calendar. These MTB trails aren't gravel-bike-friendly, but the paths and tracks in between certainly are.

Once up at the wind farm, be aware that a newer wind farm track runs in parallel to the original core path; the new track is smoother and better maintained but also slightly higher, so it offers better views. There are occasional maintenance vehicles which use the track and they won't be expecting you so ride with caution. As always be aware that huge chunks of ice can fall from the blades and seriously hurt you.

The ride uses the Aberfeldy to Dunkeld off-road route through Griffin Forest on a core path network which is signposted and generally on good tracks. Being designated core paths means they should get decent maintenance, but a couple of sections have been a bit washed out from winter rain. The route goes around Loch Kennard, but you can easily opt to detour further up to Loch Scoly, which is signposted as part of the Griffin Forest path network too.

Riding back to The Hermitage, there is a fun gravel path but watch out for walkers because the area is swarmed in the summer months; ideally have a bell or prepare to stop and start and shout politely, failing that. You can cut off to the left on to a forest track and avoid The Hermitage entirely if preferred.

Navigation

The route is an anticlockwise loop, which gets the long road section out of the way first. It also means you later enjoy the steep hairpin descent down to the small hamlet of Ballinlick; climbing up this would be painful.

Navigation can be challenging in the forests so make sure you have an OS map as well as your GPS device. The Griffin Forest path network sits between Aberfeldy and Dunkeld and is generally signposted back to Dunkeld in case of emergency. There are lots of tracks around the wind farm, but it isn't too easy to take the wrong one. Taking a map is important but bear in mind that, at the time of writing, the wind farm and associated tracks were not on the latest paper OS map – they are on digital mapping platforms though.

Facilities and refreshments

Dunkeld is getting a bit of a reputation as a foodie destination, making it a great place to start the ride. **The Aran Bakery** is run by a former *Great British Bake Off* contestant and has fantastic food selection. A drink and some food on the terrace by the river at **The Taybank** in Dunkeld is always a highlight; failing that, the fish and chip shop is worth a stop. At Grandtully you'll find **Iain Burnett Highland Chocolatier**, which has a shop and cafe, and **The Inn on the Tay**.

OPPOSITE ENDLESS GRAVEL TRACKS NEAR THE SUMMIT OF MEALL REAMHAR.

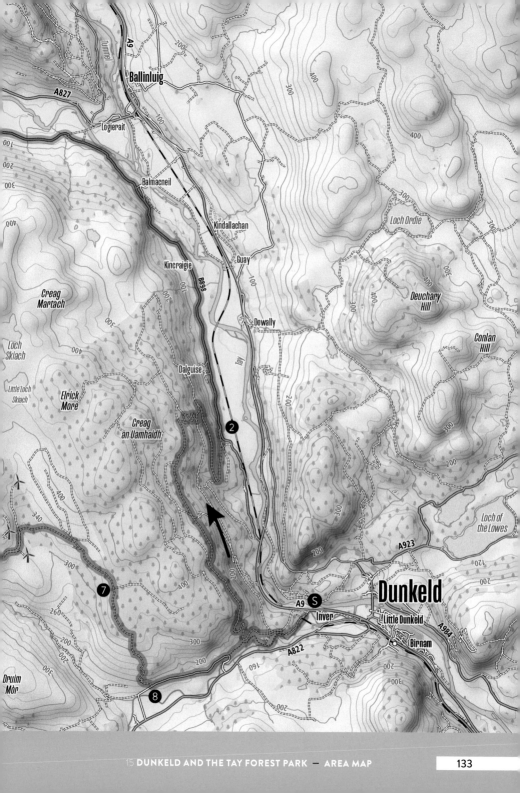

A CLASSIC BIKE IN FRONT OF A WIND TURBINE SHOT!

Bike Shops

Dunkeld has a well-stocked bike shop, **Progression Bikes** (T: 01350 727 629), which has spares and repairs and also hires bikes and equipment. It is a bit hidden through an archway off the main street.

Public transport and access

Dunkeld and Birnam railway station is next to Dunkeld and is on the main line to Inverness. This makes the train an easy option, if you can book your bike on okay.

The route starts from The Hermitage (National Trust for Scotland pay and display car park), to the west of Dunkeld.

The route

S From The Hermitage, head up into the forest on the track located just behind the paths at Ossian's Hall and the Hermitage Railway Viaduct. Head up the steady climb to the top forest road; there is an easier lower route, but you miss out on the views. The high forest road delivers a great, fast switchback descent. Both tracks eventually descend to the B898, passing around a locked barrier at the exit, so watch your speed.

2 Turn left on to the B898 and then turn left again on to the A827. Ride for 16km on a very nice section of road past idyllic isolated houses and native woodlands. In spring, the bluebells alone are worth visiting the area for. In Grandtully there is a nice pub, campsite and a fancy chocolate shop with a small chocolate-based cafe.

3 The route turns off the A827 along a narrow road signposted *St Mary's Church*. Soon after the church you reach Pitcairn Farm and the road ends; a track with a bumpy, cobbled surface now heads uphill. It is muddy in places so in winter you can continue on the A827 and take the main forest access track further along before Aberfeldy.

4 Once into the forest, the track has been affected by water damage so there is a bit of technical riding in places, but there is always a rideable line choice. Join the well-maintained and smooth gravel road. This accesses the main forest, wind farm

A FUN DESCENT AFTER PASSING LOCH KENNARD WITH THE VIEWS GETTING MORE DRAMATIC.

and a quarry so is well used by works vehicles but it is a pleasant ride. It gradually climbs up into the forest and at the high point a recently cleared site has opened up great views.

5 At Loch Kennard keep right; another climb starts as you leave the water behind. A long, fast and super-fun descent drops you down before a short climb leads to the wind farm.

6 At the wind farm you can either follow the original track (as is shown on the map and in the GPX file) or follow the wind farm track that runs in parallel to the original track but is smoother and, being higher, has better views. Finally, the tracks merge and you head back down into the forest again.

7 A right turn takes you off on to a slightly less used core path; it passes a couple of wonderfully remote houses before steeply zigzagging down to the road.

8 Turn left on to the road. At the first corner turn left on to a path back to The Hermitage; this path is great on drop bars but it can get busy with walkers, so watch your speed. (Bear in mind that Rumbling Bridge – which is the shortest alternative route avoiding this busy section of path – has been closed for some time so a longer road detour is needed if you want to avoid the crowds on this section.) Stop at The Hermitage for a look around – it is a beautiful place – before rolling back down to the start.

Other routes or attractions in the area

This route easily links on to the vast number of tracks in the Aberfeldy area. You could also head over the A9 to explore the Loch of the Lowes area with a combination of quiet roads and nice gravel. The Perthshire Gravel website has some other recommendations for routes in the area, mostly on the eastern side of the A9.

www.perthshiregravel.com

THE TRACK LEADS THE EYE UP TO GEALLAIG HILL
(ROUTE 19a).

CAIRNGORMS – DEESIDE

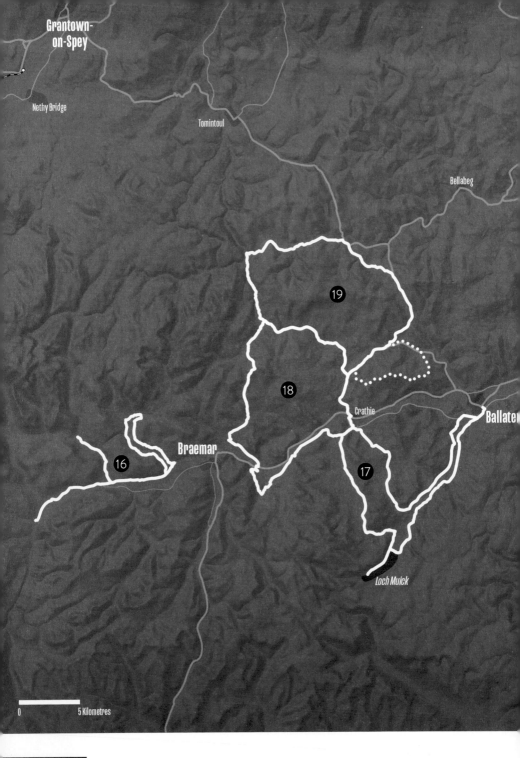

Grantown-
on-Spey

Nethy Bridge

Tomintoul

Bellabeg

19

18

Crathie

Ballater

Braemar

16

17

Loch Muick

0   5 Kilometres

CAIRNGORMS
– DEESIDE

———

Deeside and the eastern Cairngorms have some of the best and most adventurous gravel riding in the UK; the moorland tracks literally glisten from white quartz sand leading you like a fairy tale into the mountains. Their smooth surface is perfect for exploring fast and far in this sprawling wild area, this is especially helpful as the eastern Cairngorms are not that accessible by car or train so longer routes make sense.

The four routes selected are all amazing riding; three of them were deliberately selected to be in close proximity to each other so they can be all interlinked, the intention being that you can stack them up to create longer rides whether bikepacking or just for a longer day out. They also continue on to connect to longer routes like the outer loop of The Cairngorms Loop, which is mostly all rideable on a gravel bike.

The area is an iconic Scottish landscape; this is no doubt why the royal family bought the Balmoral Estate here back in the nineteenth century. The natural Cairngorms landscape brings to mind enchanting and aromatic pine forests punctuated by glimpses of snow-topped mountains on the main Cairngorm plateau. Rivers like the Dee and its cascading tributaries give the area a pure, very natural feel. Overhead it's not unusual to spot golden eagles, while in the forests capercaillies are rare but unmistakeable if spotted. The vast National Trust for Scotland nature reserve around Mar Lodge is a real highlight and well worth a visit to experience the unparalleled setting.

The main towns of Braemar and Ballater are great places to stop overnight or just for a wander or food and coffee.

16 LINN OF DEE, GLEN LUI AND LINN OF QUOICH
51KM/32 MILES

Introduction

This ride is superb; what makes it so special is the mountain backdrop and the setting among Caledonian pine forest on the Mar Lodge Estate National Nature Reserve. It is a remarkable place to ride gravel bikes. The route heads up and back down the same glens, but don't let that put you off.

The local area

While most of the other routes in the book are loops, this one is an exception for good reason. It is on good quality gravel and lets you explore up and down three of the most peaceful and scenic glens in the Cairngorms – Glen Quoich, Glen Lui and Deeside. The Mar Lodge Estate is at the heart of this ride – it is owned by the National Trust for Scotland and is managed as a nature reserve. The trust describes it as a wildlife wonderland; four of the five tallest mountains in the UK are also within the estate.

This really has to be the most naturally beautiful place in Scotland. The forests here are the kind where on a sunny day the pine smells sweet and the world shrinks to what's in front of your wheel. It is one of the best-preserved areas of the Cairngorms, lined with ancient Caledonian pine forest and with very limited development. Watch out for all the iconic species of mammals, including red squirrels and pine martens, and a great diversity of birds.

The huge and imposing Mar Lodge is actually available to book as accommodation; with a big group it's not too expensive and a truly unique experience. If you do stay, try to get a look

OPPOSITE THE RIVER CROSSING AT THE UPPER END OF GLEN QUOICH – NOT ONE FOR WET WEATHER.

DISTANCE **51km/32 miles** ━ ASCENT **392m/1,286ft** ━ OFF-ROAD **80%**
START/FINISH **Linn of Dee car park** ━ START/FINISH GRID REF **NO 063898**
SATNAV **AB35 5YB** ━ GPS **56.9898, -3.5437** ━ MAP OS **Landranger 43,**
Braemar & Blair Atholl (1:50,000)

GRAVEL SCALE
1 2 3 4 5

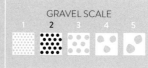

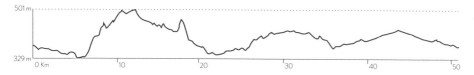

501 m

329 m

0 Km ····· 10 ····· 20 ····· 30 ····· 40 ····· 50

GRAVEL RIDES SCOTLAND

inside the Stag Ballroom; be warned it's not a place for vegans, nor for the faint of heart. The ballroom is truly bizarre and straight out of a Tim Burton movie because it is decorated with 2,430 stag skulls. If that sounds like a lot, just wait until you see it. It contrasts poignantly with the living nature outside and illustrates the history of this grand shooting lodge.

Route overview

This is a flexible route that can be done in any order or combination and, because you return the same way, you can simply go as far as you like. There are a few other tracks and smooth paths you can see in the area, but they are limited and don't add much. For example, there is also another track linking Glen Quoich and Glen Lui, but it is rougher than the others on this route so has been left out to keep the technical grade low. The paths extending on at the ends of Glen Lui and Deeside are mountain biking terrain and in places long hike-a-bikes, so don't be tempted to take a gravel bike further unless you have a love for underbiking.

As mentioned, the route can be done in any order or combination; it is included in what felt the most logical combination to minimise retracing your steps too much.

The Glen Quoich and Linn of Quoich loop has two sizable river crossings which will require very careful consideration before setting out with any rain forecast or after a period of wet weather. In wet weather, avoid the track on the eastern side of Glen Quoich, as it can get muddy and will be hard work on most gravel bike tyres; the western side of the glen is on a much better surfaced, but still fun, track, so stick to an out-and-back if unsure. The rest of the route is on superb gravel.

Navigation

The route sections can be done in any order or combination. As the sections are mostly out-and-back, navigation is simple – you'll find it hard to get lost on this one. However, still take a map as it's useful to know where it is best to turn back.

Facilities and refreshments

There are no services on the route other than a toilet and an information hut in the car park at the Linn of Dee (luckily in separate buildings). The nearest food offering is in Braemar, which has a great selection of places to eat and a good size local store. **The Bothy** is always a great stop for coffee or for an evening meal try the fancy **Fife Arms** (the bar menu is probably the best bet).

OPPOSITE A WET RIDE NEAR THE LINN OF DEE WITH A PERFECT BACKDROP.

16 **LINN OF DEE, GLEN LUI AND LINN OF QUOICH**   143

Carn
Crom

Luibeg Burn

Derry Burn

Meall an
Lundain

800
900
700
600
800
520
700
600

7 Derry Lodge
Luibeg

Creagan
nan Gabhar

G l e n   L u i

Lui Water

Sgòr
Dubh

Sgòr Mòr

Càrn an'Ic
Duibhe

Càrn
Mòr

8

Linn of Dee **S**

Dee

Dee

White
Bridge

Geldie Burn

Càrn Na Moine

9

Càrn
Liath

Bynack Burn

MORE BREATHTAKING VIEWS ALONG GLEN LUI.

Bike shops
Braemar Mountain Sports
(T: 01339 741 242) has some
hire bikes; it isn't a bike shop
as such, but they might be able
to help. Otherwise try **Cycle
Highlands** (T: 01339 755 864)
or the smaller **Bike Station**
(T: 01339 754 004) in Ballater.

Public transport and access
Unfortunately, no train stations
are within a practical distance of
the route. Park at the National
Trust for Scotland Linn of Dee
car park (parking charge) –
it does get busy in the summer,
so get there early if you can.

The route

S Start with the Linn of Quoich and Glen Quoich (eastern) loop.
From the car park turn left for a spin along the single-track
road, watching out for red squirrels. You can detour off this
road to see Mar Lodge itself.

2 Once the road ends, you pass a car park (which makes a good
alternative starting point). Cross the Quoich Water on the new
bridge (it was rebuilt in 2019) – this is the start of the gravel.
This track on the eastern side of Quoich Water is rougher and
best left for drier weather. It is muddy in places but other than
one short steep section to a river crossing it is a lot of fun and
has stunning views.

3 There is only one real junction as you skirt the edge of the
forest; navigation is straightforward for this first track.

4 A steeper section on loose stone marks the arrival of the first
river crossing. In all but the wettest conditions this should be
safe to cross. Dry your feet and turn left on to a less distinct
track which goes up and down a bit before heading left to reach
the next river crossing, which is wide but again not too deep
unless in spate.

TYPICAL SCOTTISH WEATHER OF SUNSHINE, SHOWERS AND SNOW ON THE TOPS ALONG THE GELDIE BURN.

⑤ The track follows the river; watch out for swimming spots in the river on hot days.

⑥ Once back on the single-track road, retrace your steps. Just before you reach the Linn of Dee car park turn right, passing to the side of a locked gate, on a very appealing looking section of gravel track along Glen Lui.

⑦ Enjoy the gravel and just ride until the track ends or your legs tire. Then turn around and enjoy a different set of views.

⑧ Once near the road again you can take a track into the back of the Linn of Dee car park, or just rejoin the road and turn right. The Deeside track is simple to find. Follow the road until it curves sharply towards a bridge over the gorge. Instead of following the road, keep straight ahead and enjoy more epic gravel that stretches out before you.

⑨ Again, just follow the track, this time until you reach a (currently disused) bothy. Then just retrace your steps back to the start.

Other routes or attractions in the area

This ride doesn't naturally extend to include another route in this book, as all the obvious extensions are walking paths or mountain bike routes. A popular mountain bike option is to carry on south through Glen Tilt to Blair Atholl; there is a debate whether this is rideable on a gravel bike as it is mostly MTB terrain for the first part.

17 BALLATER, BALMORAL AND LOCH MUICK
57KM/35 MILES

Introduction

This route is on perfect gravel with one steep and rough section off the bike; otherwise, it is smooth quartz sand tracks, all in the spectacular shadow of Lochnagar. The ride really packs some punch; even the optional out-and-back along Loch Muick is cracking riding.

The local area

The area around Loch Muick is rightly recognised as one of the classic Scottish landscapes. The ancient pine forests along the River Dee and the white quartz tracks off into the hills deliver endless adventure. This route is almost all within the confines of the Balmoral Estate and it is easy to see why the royals fell in love with the area – with eagles overhead, babbling burns with pools and gorges and then Loch Muick itself sitting in front of the lofty peak of Lochnagar. For many, Lochnagar is a favourite mountain, and this route gives great views of the peak. While Loch Muick is inviting for a cold-water dip, given its elevation it's best left for a sunny day.

As you might expect, Balmoral is a well-managed estate and the tracks are generally great; you'll often see smart estate vehicles cruising about and when the royal family are in residence it's common to see Range Rovers with security detail parked up in some unexpected lay-bys nearer the main estate houses.

In summer this area gets busier and busier, but don't despair as most people generally stay around Loch Muick near the car park. The ride starts in Ballater; there is ample parking and there are great food and drink options too.

OPPOSITE POSSIBLY THE BEST GRAVEL TRACK IN SCOTLAND IN THE SHADOW OF LOCHNAGAR.

DISTANCE **57km/35 miles** — ASCENT **760m/2,493ft** — OFF-ROAD **60%**
START/FINISH **Ballater** — START/FINISH GRID REF **NO 371957**
SATNAV **AB35 5QP** — GPS **57.0481, -3.0384** — MAP OS Landranger 44,
Ballater & Glen Clova (1:50,000)

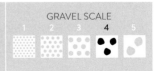

GRAVEL SCALE

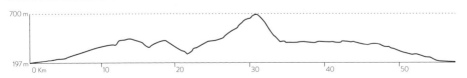

GRAVEL RIDES SCOTLAND

If you opt to ride the out-and-back on the western shore of Loch Muick you'll find Glas-allt-Shiel, a Victorian lodge on the Balmoral Estate. In its present form it was built in 1868 by Queen Victoria, who called it Glassalt; she also called it her 'widow's house', as she could escape there from the world following the death of her husband, Albert. There is a rather classy bothy next to the house.

Route overview

To get the negatives out of the way and to be very clear – this route has one very technical rough section (around 1 or 2 kilometres long) that most riders will have to walk for; however, the tracks before and after are such immensely good gravel that it is worth the hike and brief struggle. Also, on the tracks heading north to Easter Balmoral there have been reports of two locked gates. Luckily they are not deer gates, so they are easy enough for most riders to overcome, except for those riding ebikes or for less able riders. For some reason these were not encountered when researching the ride, but it is worth noting. These two factors combine to give the ride a grade of 4 out of 5, but it is a 1 out of 5 on all other sections. The out-and-back along the western shore of Loch Muick is a great little add-on too – the lochside beach makes a perfect picnic spot. The tracks over to Balmoral are very remote and open to the elements, so be well prepared.

The route starts at Ballater; this saves driving out to Loch Muick and adds in a nice section of gravel and single-track road. The car park at Loch Muick also gets busy; there is ample parking in Ballater.

Navigation

The suggested ride direction is anticlockwise – this way around means that a short (around 1 or 2 kilometres) very rough section (which very few gravel riders will stay on the bike for) is a descent; you might opt to reverse the route and do this section as an uphill push so as to enjoy the long gravel descent. This depends on whether you like (and have the skill for) technical descents.

Navigation is pretty straight-forward with very few obvious options to go wrong. The forest around Balmoral is the most confusing part. ScotWays signs do help in places, but there are no waymarked routes here.

Facilities and refreshments

Ballater tailors to a well-healed tourist market and is especially popular with Americans; as a result, it has lots of good places to eat.

In the car park beside Balmoral, conveniently located at around halfway around the loop, there are toilets and a visitor centre that sells ice cream and drinks. The cafe within Balmoral needs a ticket for entrance. The Royal Lochnagar Distillery is on the route just before Balmoral, but unless you want a tasting or a bottle of fine single malt mid-ride the options are limited here.

There are toilets and a visitor centre by the car park at Loch Muick, but no food or drink available.

OPPOSITE QUARTZ GRAVEL ON THE TRACK TOWARDS EASTER BALMORAL.

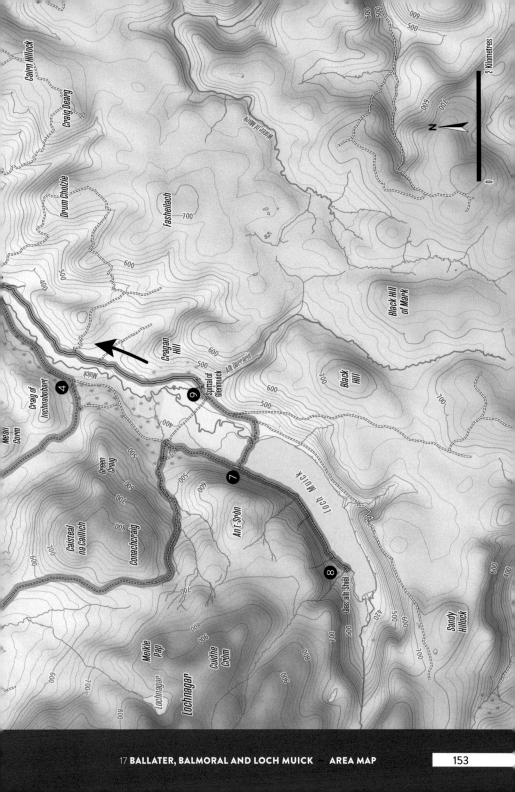

THE KINESIS TRIPSTER ATR IN ITS NATURAL ENVIRONMENT LOOKING TOWARDS THE BALMORAL ESTATE.

Bike shops

There are two good bike shops in Ballater, making another good reason to start the route here: **Cycle Highlands** (T: 01339 755 864) and the smaller **Bike Station** (T: 01339 754 004).

Public transport and access

Unfortunately, no train stations are within a practical distance of the route. There is ample free parking in Ballater.

The route

🅢 Head out of Ballater on the road bridge over the River Dee; turn right and follow the B976 heading west. At the hamlet of Bridge of Muick, turn right staying on the B976 (the turn off here goes to Loch Muick; this is your return route).

② After about 1km you reach a five-way junction next to a red post box; take the second small road on the left. This tarmac single-track road passes native forests and rhododendrons – it makes a very pleasant section of the ride.

③ After around 3km the road curves to the left on to a narrow bridge over the River Muick to Mill of Sterin; straight ahead is a track with a no entry sign which says *locked deer gate*. Take the track straight ahead with the no entry sign (this sign is only directed at motor vehicles). Follow the track as far as an old estate building at Inchnabobart.

④ Turn right at Inchnabobart on to a rougher grassy track (alternatively, carry on for 1.5km and take the next right turn on to smoother gravel). Either way takes you on to the high moorland track over towards Balmoral. This is superb riding with great views north to the southern Cairngorm plateau and the ever-present Lochnagar to the west. The only junction is a track heading east to Bovaglie; ignore this and continue to the small back road at Easter Balmoral.

GRAVEL RIDES SCOTLAND

CLASSIC CAIRNGORM VIEW OF THE MOUNTAINS AND NATIVE CALEDONIAN PINE.

5 Ride past the distillery and into Easter Balmoral; take the first left turn uphill past some houses and soon you are on to gravel.

6 Take the next left turn heading deep into a charming pine forest which accesses the moors again with a steady climb up. Once on the moors, enjoy the views on this perfect gravel. When you reach the summit this all changes and the track deteriorates into a horrible rough and steep descent for 1–2km; if in doubt, just walk it. It smooths out before some fun gravel paths through the woods lead to the northern tip of Loch Muick.

7 Here there is an option for an out-and-back on a good track along the western shore of Loch Muick to Glas-allt-Shiel, the grand hunting lodge.

8 The loch makes an enchanting spot for some lunch or to sit down on the peaceful rust-coloured sandy beach. It is a popular wild camping spot; the rangers have been kept busy here in the past clearing up after careless campers. Bear this in mind if you're thinking of sleeping in the area. The section across the northern end of Loch Muick can be muddy – detour further north on a gravel path if you prefer. A final gravel blast dodging the walkers leads you back towards Loch Muick car park.

9 From the car park enjoy a fun warm-down 14km ride back down the tarmac road to Ballater.

Other routes or attractions in the area

This route is designed to link into **18 Invercauld and the River Gairn** (pages 157–163) to carry on further north. The two routes use the same track for a short time near Balmoral, so can easily be connected.

Knock Castle, a ruined tower house, is just off the route near Ballater. It is typical of the traditional type of residence of a laird and is the ancestral seat of Lady Krisztina de Varga of Knock.

18 INVERCAULD AND THE RIVER GAIRN
45KM/28 MILES

Introduction

A classic Cairngorms gravel ride – it is all on good quality tracks and takes you right into a beautiful area of forest and open moorland. It has one beast of a climb up to almost 750 metres in height, delivering an amazing long descent into the grounds of Invercauld House.

The local area

The route is mostly on the Invercauld Estate, which is a vast, traditional Highland estate. Owned by the Farquharson family since the fifteenth century, the estate is run mostly for shooting things but they also run the nearby caravan park and Braemar Castle too. Some of the grouse moors here have been let to the Queen for many years and it was a favourite 'resort' of Queen Victoria. The estate covers a mind-blowing 108,000 acres and is listed as employing just 26 people. In May 2021 local police reported a that a golden eagle was found 'illegally and intentionally poisoned' on the estate, but no one to date has been identified as being responsible. It sadly wasn't the first incident of this type in this part of the Cairngorms according to the RSPB, a reminder that there is still a way to go in conservation efforts.

The route crosses the River Dee on the historic Bridge of Dee into the beautiful forests around the fringes of the Balmoral Estate. There are actually two bridges here – the Bridge of Dee, dating back to around 1752 and built by Major Caulfeild as part of the military road from Perthshire through the mountains to

OPPOSITE THE FINAL CLIMB IS A KILLER BUT THE DESCENT WILL BLOW YOU AWAY.

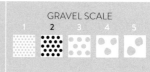

DISTANCE **45km/28 miles** — ASCENT **762m/2,500ft** — OFF-ROAD **80%**
START/FINISH **Invercauld Bridge car park** — START/FINISH GRID REF
NO 188913 — SATNAV **AB35 5TW** — GPS **57.0057, -3.3385**
MAP OS Landranger 36, Grantown & Aviemore; 37, Strathdon & Alford;
43, Braemar & Blair Atholl; 44, Ballater & Glen Clova (1:50,000)

GRAVEL SCALE

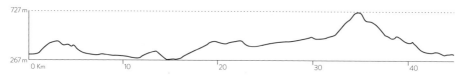

Speyside. It wasn't used for very long as Queen Victoria bought Balmoral and the military road was apparently diverted so Invercauld Bridge was built.

Ballochbuie Forest is a classic Scottish pine forest with gravel riding on good tracks. The track gets out of the trees long enough to offer some views before dropping back down to the River Dee.

Later on in the route, a huge but rewarding climb gets you up to the shoulder of Culardoch, a 900-metre peak, into the skies where the remaining eagles dare to fly past. It's not quite Munro height, but the ridgetop track is impressive, looks out over open moorland and feels miles from civilization. At the start of this climb is a modern timber-framed shooting shelter; it has an interesting design with odd-shaped windows and a grass roof. It looks rather luxurious; sadly it isn't a bothy.

Route overview

This route is all pretty consistently on tracks, but the gravel isn't always perfectly smooth with rougher sections on the descent from Loch Builg and up the main climb, making it a solid grade 2 for technicality. From Invercauld, the area through the forest is lovely but can get confusing as it's a uniform pine forest. The track heading west from the B976 along the River Gairn (the track eventually reaches Glen Avon) is sublime gravel riding; don't be tempted to take an earlier turn-off from the B976 into a small woodland as it's not great riding. Along the River Gairn there is a shallow ford of a burn – this shouldn't present issues unless it is in deep spate. Around halfway through the route there are two remote buildings at Corndavon – once a royal shooting lodge and staff quarters and later part of it was a bothy. They are now just locked and boarded up.

Navigation
The route is best done anti-clockwise as the main climb is rideable and the descent back down to Invercauld is simply stunning; the perfect end to the route. Navigation is pretty straightforward with limited junctions, other than the various tracks in Ballochbuie Forest; any wrong turn needs catching early as you are already in a remote area.

Facilities and refreshments
There are no real services on the route, except for when the visitor centre is open in the car park at Balmoral; it serves basic drinks and ice creams and has toilets. The start at Invercauld is not too far from Braemar, where there are multiple services and food options.

Bike shops
Braemar Mountain Sports (T: 01339 741 242) has some hire bikes; it isn't a bike shop as such, but they might be able to help. Otherwise try **Cycle Highlands** (T: 01339 755 864) or the smaller **Bike Station** (T: 01339 754 004) in Ballater.

1 STARTING OUT ON THE FINAL CLIMB.

2 THE FIRST SECTION OF THE EPIC DESCENT TO INVERCAULD.

3 LOW LIGHT PANNING AS THE ROUTE LEAVES THE RIVER GAIRN.

4 DON'T GET CAUGHT OUT IN THE DARK IF TAKING ON THIS RIDE IN WINTER.

5 AUTUMN COLOURS ON THE INVERCAULD ESTATE.

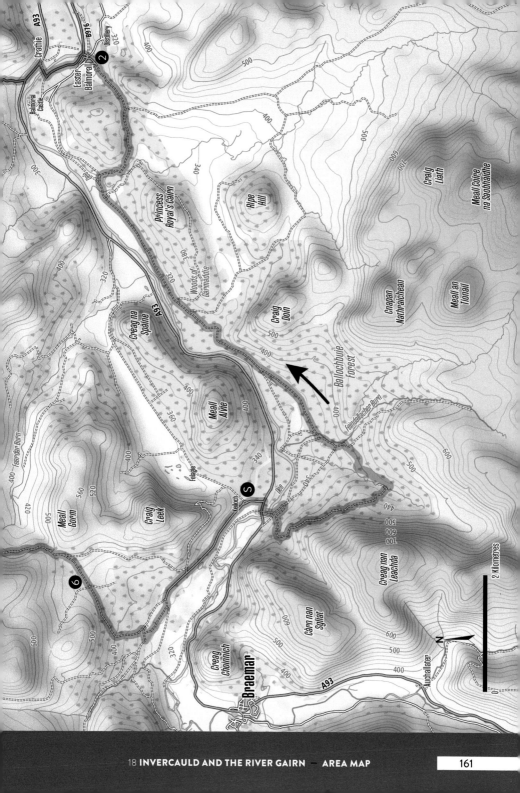

The route

S Leave the car park and head over the old Bridge of Dee and on to forest tracks. This impressive bridge is one of the bridges built for the military road in around 1752. Through the forest you will need some careful navigating. There are a few ways through; our route takes a higher track and so long as you don't head too far away from the river you will come out at Easter Balmoral.

2 From Easter Balmoral start a steep road climb heading north. The OS map shows a tempting-looking shortcut from the B976 on to the route, but this is rough and muddy; stay on the road until you reach a sandy gravel track on the left.

3 There are a few car parking spaces here where the track turns off and there is a gate to navigate. It is then smooth track all the way to the junction south of Loch Builg. You can't see the loch before you turn left. This is on coarse, but well-made, gravel.

4 The climbing really starts as you pass a modern wooden shooting hut – you know you're in for some pain! The climb is steady and never too steep, but it is relentless.

5 Once on the ridgetop the views are impressive and so is the sight of the gravel track leading the eye away south, up and down hills towards Invercauld. The track is mostly downhill to the finish; a couple of short climbs look worse than they are.

6 The final descent gives wonderful views of the Dee and up to Braemar, before diving into the trees flat-out fast. Some careful navigation is needed on estate tracks to avoid going in a circle instead of back to the start. The grounds of the imposing Invercauld House are dotted with large fir trees making a grand finish.

Public transport and access

Unfortunately, no train stations are within a practical distance of the route. The route starts at Invercauld Bridge car park (parking charge) just off the A93. If this small car park is busy, drive along to the Balmoral car park, which is also on the route. You could opt to add some road riding on the A93 and start in Braemar as well.

Other routes or attractions in the area

This route is designed to be connected with either (or both) of **17 Ballater, Balmoral and Loch Muick** (pages 149–155) and **19 Corgarff Castle and a military road** (pages 165–171), to make one long or a multi-day gravel feast. If combining this route with route 19, do so in a figure of eight, rather than just doing the outer loop, as the gravel section in the middle is superb and worth doing twice.

OPPOSITE PREPARE FOR A FEW STREAM AND RIVER SPLASHES ON THIS ROUTE.

19 CORGARFF CASTLE AND A MILITARY ROAD

43KM/27 MILES

Introduction

This ride is through an area rich in dramatic military history and passes the evocative and isolated white tower of Corgarff Castle. It crosses crumbling 250-year-old stone bridges and up to the isolated shores of Loch Builg. There is also a highly recommended optional route up along a summit ridge offering great views over the Dee Valley before a rather bumpy descent.

The local area

The dramatic Corgarff Castle is a remote white tower that wouldn't look out of place in *The Lord of the Rings*; it was built in around 1550 most likely by John Forbes of Towie (not that TOWIE) and it could fill its own book, such is its history. Early on, the castle was burnt down in a local family feud, killing all inside; it is said to be haunted. Since then, it has been a hideout for raiders, burnt down by retreating Jacobites, a military barracks, a private house and an army outpost to prevent whisky smuggling; it is currently owned by Historic Environment Scotland and operated as a museum. An entry fee is payable to visit the castle – it is worth a dedicated visit rather than a quick stop.

The fun ride along the A939 follows the route of one of Scotland's military roads, before the surface turns to gravel to continue on the route of the military road. This section includes three original stone arch bridges, each in various states of disrepair – only one is probably safe to ride over.

The route crosses three large Highland estates – Invercauld, Balmoral and Glenavon – and the area is in the Cairngorms

OPPOSITE ONE OF THE REAL CLASSIC GRAVEL SECTIONS IN SCOTLAND HEADING TOWARDS LOCH BUILG.

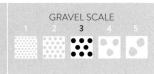

DISTANCE **43km/27 miles** ━ ASCENT **590m/1,936ft** ━ OFF-ROAD **75%**
START/FINISH **Small lay-by on the B976, north-west of Ballater**
START/FINISH GRID REF **NO 261981** ━ SATNAV **AB35 5UQ**
GPS **57.0680, -3.2204** ━ MAP **OS Landranger 36, Grantown & Aviemore; 37, Strathdon & Alford (1:50,000)**

GRAVEL SCALE
1   2   **3**   4   5

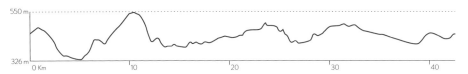

GRAVEL RIDES SCOTLAND

National Park. It is all heavily managed; unsurprisingly, the main species that flourish are the game that gets shot: black and red grouse, red deer and mountain hares. The heather is all burnt systematically to promote fresh growth for grouse, which leaves unsightly zebra-like stripes across the moor. The enchanting pine forests found along the River Dee become very sparse, replaced with desolate moorland and epic views. The vista over to the infamous Lochnagar mountain is immense – in spring it is still streaked with old snow, in late August the heather is in bloom and in late autumn, if you time a visit right, you can see the first dusting of snow on the highest peaks.

In the skies you'll see the surviving eagles and kites on most rides; you'll always see the entertaining lapwings that fly and tumble through the air like stunt pilots showing off. With gravel riding being on well-established tracks the conflict with stalking is minimal, but be aware of estate activities for your own safety.

Route overview

Deciding on a route in this region was so hard because there are so many tracks in all directions. This loop is the furthest north of the three interconnected rides in this section. This ride is rated 3 out of 5; however, in reality, it is almost all is grade 1 except for a section of singletrack around the remote Loch Builg, which sits in an elevated location. This path is about 85% rideable on a gravel bike if you have the skill and energy, and obviously much less if it is totally saturated with water. This section brings the ride's average rating to about 3 out of 5. The Loch Builg singletrack gets more and more rideable as it gets more bike traffic. If that all sounds too easy, then you're in luck because there's a very highly recommended route extension (**19a Corgarff Castle and a military road: extension**, distance: 52 kilometres, ascent: 901 metres) – it takes in a dramatic summit ridge track and the climb and descent will leave you grinning but hurting all over, even if you manage to stay on the bike.

Along the upper Builg Burn there are two medium size river crossings; while only just above the ankles in average conditions the river can rise quickly when in spate so be prepared as it is a long way to retrace your steps at this point.

Navigation

The route is probably best done in an anticlockwise direction. Without any forest the navigation is easier than most routes in this book, but only if you're on the right track. This is a remote part of the country and not somewhere to be unprepared or get lost.

Facilities and refreshments

This is a real adventure and accordingly there are no food or drink options on the route. There is a cafe called **Goodbrand and Ross** on the A939 about 2.5 kilometres from the northern end of the route. It offers a hearty full Scottish breakfast for those who are bikepacking and a gift shop in case you need a scented candle. Another option is to start further south at Balmoral, where there is a car park and a basic cafe; however, either way once on the gravel you need to be self-sufficient. To the north is also the intoxicating Whisky Castle and basic shops in Tomintoul.

Bike shops

Near Corgarff Castle you aren't too far from **Glenlivet Mountain Bike Trail Centre** (T: 07963 217 793), which has very basic spares if open. Otherwise, try **Cycle Highlands** (T: 01339 755 864) or the smaller **Bike Station** (T: 01339 754 004) in Ballater.

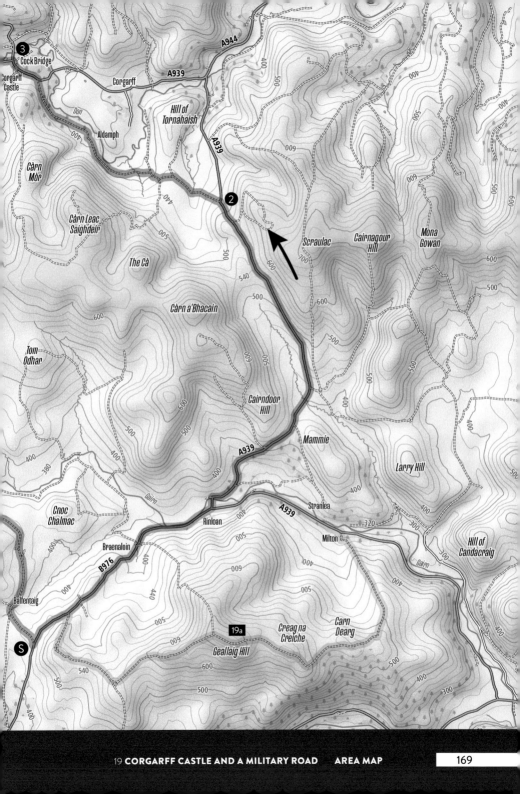

THE HILL TRACKS IN THIS PART OF THE CAIRNGORMS STRETCH IN EVERY DIRECTION.

Public transport and access

Unfortunately, no train stations are within a practical distance of the route. The route starts at a small lay-by on the B976 where the track to Glen Avon forks off on vivid orange quartz gravel. It fits about six cars; in the rare case that it is full, drop down the road to Balmoral car park.

Other routes or attractions in the area

The route extension marked on the map and with an accompanying GPX file (**19a Corgarff Castle and a military road: extension**, distance: 52 kilometres, ascent: 901 metres) is a must-ride for experienced cyclists. This is a superb detour up and along 743-metre Geallaig Hill – but be aware that it is techy riding along a broad ridge and your teeth will be shaken out on the descent.

This route connects with **18 Invercauld and the River Gairn** (pages 157–163) – routes

The route

S Start by heading north on the B976. (After around 1km the track for option **19a** heads off to the right; the track looks steep and rough but gets better – in places.) The main route joins the A939. The big climb is laid out in front of you leading off into the distance, but it isn't as bad as it looks.

2 Stay on the A939 until you reach a left fork on to a great section of gravel (this track is the original route of the military road) then rejoin the A939. (If you're hungry, detour to the east along the A939 for around 2.5km to reach Goodbrand and Ross.)

3 Turn left off the A939, following the sign for *Corgarff Castle*; you'll be able to see the large white castle as you ride past. The ride carries on along a single-track road; the tarmac finally ends at some estate buildings. The gravel track is good but does deteriorate into rougher grassy doubletrack as you approach Glen Avon.

4 The lonely lodge at Inchrory on the Avon is an impressive building, especially considering its location, but get more excited as you turn left on to some of the very best gravel riding in the Cairngorms. There are quite a few river and smaller burn crossings coming up so you'll need to accept some wet socks as the track undulates alongside the Builg Burn.

SCOTTISH-BUILT BIKES ON SCOTTISH TRAILS.

5 The track climbs steadily up to Loch Builg; the last two river crossings are the trickiest. Where the track turns to a wet path is particularly challenging. The singletrack starts off boggy, with wheel-sucking puddles, and you'll be on and off the bike around the loch, but it doesn't last long in the grand scheme of things. In wet conditions the small lochan to the south can flood over the path and you'll do well to keep feet dry.

6 Once at the deer fence past the small lochan, keep left and follow this perfect, smooth gravel track back east towards the start. You pass two estate buildings; neither are a bothy. This section follows the same route as part of **18 Invercauld and the River Gairn** (pages 157–163) – it gets included twice because it is that good!

7 Cross the River Gairn then fork right to return to the start. This section of quartz sand is absolutely perfect for gravel bikes.

18 and **19** together are best done in a figure of eight, rather than just doing the outer loop, as the gravel section in the middle is superb and worth doing twice.

Alternatively, there are awesome tracks heading north through Speyside. You can head north from this route through Glen Avon to Tomintoul, then detour through Glenlivet and via various Speyside distilleries to Buckie on the coast. It was a really hard decision to not include a Speyside route in the book, but I wanted to prioritise achievable routes that are closer together.

Locally it seems like almost every hill has a 4x4 track to the top. Quite a few are part of complete loops and most that are marked as tracks on OS maps are 80% rideable because they get used by estate vehicles; however, they are steep so the time spent off the bike will vary depending on your motivation and fitness.

THE LONG GRAVEL STRETCH ALONGSIDE LOCH ERICHT
(ROUTE 20)

CAIRNGORMS
– AVIEMORE

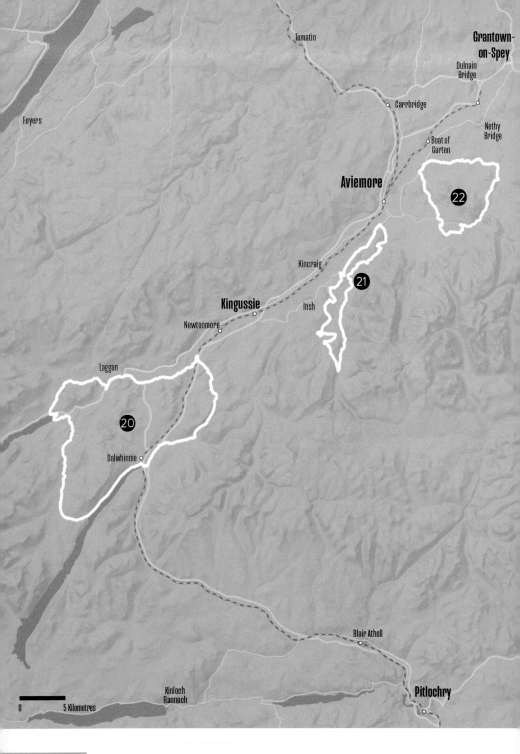

Tomatin

Grantown-
on-Spey

Dulnain
Bridge

Foyers

Carrbridge

Boat of
Garten

Nethy
Bridge

Aviemore

22

Kincraig

21

Kingussie

Insh

Newtonmore

Laggan

20

Dalwhinnie

Blair Atholl

Pitlochry

Kinloch
Rannoch

0   5 Kilometres

CAIRNGORMS – AVIEMORE

———

The western Cairngorms around Aviemore is one of the best-known parts of Scotland and a great gravel destination, famed for its easy access to the Cairngorm Plateau, wildlife-rich native pine forests, the stunning Loch Morlich and the Cairngorm Mountain ski resort on the slopes of Cairn Gorm. The A9 trunk road makes the area very accessible by car from the south, but Aviemore also has a railway station with direct trains to Inverness, Edinburgh, Glasgow and beyond. Easy access by train opens the possibility of epic one-way trips too.

Aviemore is a great base with a wide range of facilities and a growing number of good cafe options; bikepackers passing through the Cairngorms will all recommend the fish and chip shop to the south of town.

To the north-east is the wild Abernethy National Nature Reserve near Loch Garten, while to the south of Aviemore is Glen Feshie which is undergoing quite a rewilding transformation – the results of the last decade speak for themselves. The Glenfeshie estate is a centrepiece of the vast land holding of Wildland Ltd, who are now the largest private landowner in Scotland. Loch Morlich, Loch an Eilein and Loch Ericht are all wonderful spots passed on these routes.

20 DALWHINNIE, LOCH ERICHT AND LAGGAN
68KM/42 MILES

Introduction

This route gets into some remote and wild country and feels way longer than 68 kilometres. It should be on all riders' bucket lists as it follows remote lochs, castles, towering Munros and a beautiful river gorge with wild swimming spots.

The local area

Dalwhinnie sits just north of the Drumochter Pass on the A9; the village is notable for Dalwhinnie Distillery with its iconic pagoda towers. This is the highest distillery in Scotland and, much like its geographic location, it produces a smoother whisky which is a nice compromise between Speyside and the intense smoky and peaty whiskies of western Scotland. Dalwhinnie is the access point to one of the most scenic but accessible wild areas of the Central Highlands: Loch Ericht and the Ben Alder peaks. This area around Ben Alder has long been a mountain biker's favourite – there are a few singletrack loops of the mountain, with varying amounts of hike-a-bike.

The area around Loch Pattack is breathtaking and a popular area for wild camping while hiking up the neighbouring Munros, but watch out for the wild ponies who live here. Most campers tend to stick around the now disused bothy (it is closed due to asbestos) and the area is sadly dotted with abandoned bikes.

After you negotiate a muddy section, you reach an old wooden bridge and follow the River Pattack deeper into the towering forests of the Ardverikie Estate. Ardverikie House

OPPOSITE THE CLIMB UP TOWARDS LOCH PATTACK.

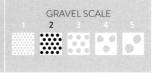

DISTANCE **68km/42 miles** — ASCENT **673m/2,208ft** — OFF-ROAD **80%**
START/FINISH **Dalwhinnie** — START/FINISH GRID REF **NN 637842**
SATNAV **PH19 1AF** — GPS **56.9290, -4.2412** — MAP OS Landranger 35, Kingussie & Monadhliath Mountains; 42, Glen Garry & Loch Rannoch (1:50,000)

GRAVEL SCALE
1   2   3   4   5

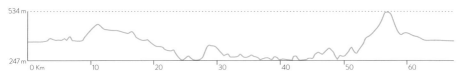

LOCH PATTACK AT DAWN AFTER A WILD CAMP.

Navigation

The best direction for this route is clockwise, as this gets the best section done first and you can decide how long or short to make it once you reach the A889 near Laggan. The tracks used follow the sides of lochs or are generally easy to follow. However, the navigation is a little more complex on the eastern section near Loch Cuaich. The route is entirely out in the open; there aren't any confusing plantation forests to navigate.

and its surroundings have appeared on TV and in films, as it is an archetypal Scottish castle and lochside setting.

The route takes in a spectacular section of track north from Loch Laggan with views over to Ardverikie House and the Munros of Càrn Liath and Creag Meagaidh. This track meets the old military road between Ruthven Barracks and Fort Augustus – you can feel and see the weight of history along this section, mostly from the remaining stone bridges.

The route passes lots of tempting of wild swimming spots, such as the shallow shores of Loch Pattack, deep pools in the lower River Pattack and the isolated Loch Cuaich on the last section. The River Pattack is dramatic; a detour to see the Linn of Pattack is worth doing; but don't ride on the path too near the edge.

Route overview

Don't underestimate this ride – it deserves an epic tagline. The route is varied and includes literally every surface from main roads to muddy singletrack, and every type of gravel in between. The track along Loch Ericht was made for gravel bikes; as you climb to Loch Pattack, you'll feel it in your legs, but the orange sandy track leads the eye up to the surrounding Munros, providing one of the

GRAVEL RIDES SCOTLAND

RED GRAVEL AFTER LEAVING LOCH ERICHT BEHIND.

best views in this book. There are only two sections along the route which are normally wet and muddy. Firstly, the section of track from the northern end of Loch Pattack along the River Pattack; in all but the driest conditions there will be some bog jumping mixed in with some riding for around 1.5 kilometres, until it becomes a good track again at the first bridge. Secondly, it can be wet at the pass just before Loch Cuaich and alongside the loch itself. These two sections combined are around 3 or 4 kilometres, so don't be put off by them. The section to Loch Cuaich can be bypassed by taking the cycle path along the A9; the Loch Cuaich section is tough with tired legs, but it's well worth the effort to get into the lonelier hills. It uses a nice, new, smooth hydroelectric track to get back down to the A9.

While the loop commits you to a minimum of around 50 kilometres, if your legs are tired you can take the A889 or the A9 cycle path for an easy spin back to the start. The A86 isn't the best road; you can avoid most of this by using the singletrack at the Laggan Wolftrax Centre, as detailed in the directions and on the GPX, or diverting earlier in the route at Crathie and following the back road to Laggan. The A889 is better than the A86, but still has quite a few fast cars.

Facilities and refreshments

The route is very wild, and you are fully committed to a big loop with no real shortcuts until you reach the A889, so be prepared. The **Snack Shack** in Dalwhinnie serves a hearty Scottish menu.

A stop at the **Laggan Wolftrax Centre** is worthwhile to visit the cafe and to add some smooth singletrack; check the opening hours first, as they do vary. If you stay on the back road heading east at Crathie you reach the **Laggan Coffee Bothy and Gallery**, a great little stop. On the A889 after the Wolftrax singletrack rejoins the road is **Caoldair Coffee and Craft Shop** – this little gem is the last food stop before you get back to the start.

1 LOCH PATTACK AT DUSK. **2** HEADING DOWN ALONG GLEN PATTACK.

Bike shops

The nearest bike shops are to the north of the route in Kingussie: **Wee Bike Hub** (T: 01528 544 751) and **Bothy Bikes** (T: 01479 810 111). (The bike shop at the Laggan Wolftrax Centre was closed at the time of writing.)

Public transport and access

Dalwhinnie railway station is on the main line to Inverness; you can be inventive by extending this route to the north and catching the train back from Kingussie. Alternatively, there is some on-street parking in Dalwhinnie.

S From Dalwhinnie, go through the tunnel under the railway line then follow the superb Loch Ericht gravel track heading south.

2 After passing a couple of impressive lodge buildings, take a steep, shady track to the right just before the huge Ben Alder Lodge. As you climb higher the track starts to become a unique reddy orange colour due to the mineral soil used. Follow the track past a small pine forest and along the shore of Loch Pattack.

3 Next up is a wet section of track which you will no doubt curse. It is rideable in sections but will depend on recent weather. As this track gets more use, there is a singletrack line that does seem to help smooth it out in places. After about 1.5km an old wooden bridge over the river signals the track becoming well surfaced again.

4 Continue past a new hydroelectric scheme and follow the pipeline beside the river. Near the end of the track there is a signpost to the *Linn of Pattack* – it's worth a stop and a short walk to view the waterfall.

5 After reaching a farm, turn left and head through the forest and along the end of Loch Laggan. Cross the River Pattack to reach the lodge house and gates for Kinloch Laggan on the A86. Turn left for a very short stint on the A86.

6 From the A86 turn right on to a steep gravel track heading north. This is dramatic gravel riding with epic views as you climb up. The track deteriorates in the forest but is still fine for a gravel bike.

RIDING ALONG LOCH ERICHT NEAR DALWHINNIE.

⑦ The track merges with a tarmac section of one of General Wade's military roads; to the left is the infamous Corrieyairack Pass and a bothy. This pass is rightly famous for bikepackers, as it opens up so many options to the north. Head east on the tarmac, passing a vast new substation and pylons.

⑧ The route detours to the Laggan Wolftrax Centre for a coffee and some easy singletrack, but you can easily keep on the A86 or stay further north at Crathie and go via Laggan if preferred. From the end of the singletrack, go through Gorstean car park then turn right on to the A86.

⑨ Turn right on to the A889, passing the delightful Caoldair Coffee and Craft Shop. Turn left on to the back road at Catlodge; follow this until you reach the A9.

⑩ Turn left on to the cycle path just before the A9. Head north before turning across the A9, crossing with care at the signpost for *Phoines Lodge*. (The track takes you up to a pass and eventually on to Loch Cuaich on a good track, but it is soft ground at the pass and in places alongside the loch so best avoided in wet conditions. Alternatively, you can opt to head south on the A9 cycle path to avoid this rougher section (and climb).)

⑪ Ride past Phoines Lodge which has lapwings on the gateposts; you need some careful navigation here to stay on the right track. The track can get wet in pieces, especially alongside Loch Cuaich. Cross the dam at Loch Cuaich then descend on the track alongside the aqueduct back to the A9 and on to Dalwhinnie.

Other routes or attractions in the area

This route is designed to be made shorter if needed once you reach the A889 – if you have the legs do the full loop but otherwise you can 'escape' back south. The route can extend in literally every direction. To the west is the Corrieyairack Pass to Fort Augustus. To the north-east is the Glen Feshie area accessed from Kingussie (see **21 Glen Feshie and Loch an Eilein** (pages 185–191)). To the south you can carry on to Rannoch, although the paths around Ben Alder are not gravel-bike-friendly so you need to head north of Loch Laggan and then west to pick up the track heading south to Corrour railway station. To the south-east you can pick up the Gaick Pass track from the A9.

21 GLEN FESHIE AND LOCH AN EILEIN
46KM/29 MILES

Introduction
This route is one of the best rides in Scotland for its scenery and natural setting. It passes the best views in the Cairngorms; it has steep climbs, technical but mostly rideable singletrack sections and beautiful lochs. Just ride it, but please, please respect this sensitive natural setting and think twice about wild camping in some spots.

The local area
Loch an Eilein (loch of the island) is at the start of the route, with its island castle spotted as you end the ride. The castle was built as a place of safety against marauding neighbouring clans, who used the so-called Thieves' Road along the eastern shores of the loch to descend on Strathspey in search of plunder. This area is part of the estate of Rothiemurchus – the estate promotes access and encourages visitors to the area but they caution that the area is sensitive and needs respect, so they ask that visitors consider not wild camping in certain areas. Rothiemurchus Forest is important not just for the trees but for the wonderfully rich network of habitats that it contains; it is very wild, as soon as you leave the loch and the paddleboards behind. In peak summer season Loch an Eilein is a bit of a circus and you might consider avoiding this section. The estate tries to manage the visitors by promoting specific sites, such as Loch an Eilein and Loch Morlich, to leave the various protected species in peace in the areas in between.

Further south, Glen Feshie is undergoing a transformation.

OPPOSITE AN OLD BUILDING IN GLEN FESHIE.

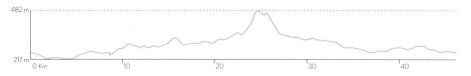

| DISTANCE **46km/29 miles** — ASCENT **354m/1,161ft** — OFF-ROAD **50%** |
| START/FINISH **Loch an Eilein car park** — START/FINISH GRID REF **NH 897085** |
| SATNAV **PH22 1QP** — GPS **57.1541 , -3.8250** — MAP **OS Landranger 35, Kingussie & Monadhliath Mountains; 36, Grantown & Aviemore (1:50,000)** |

GRAVEL SCALE

1   2   **3**   4   5

482 m

217 m

0 Km   10   20   30   40

A SIGNPOST TO SHOW THE RIVER FESHIE CROSSING.

Navigation

This route is best ridden anticlockwise. It is challenging to navigate in places with a lot of criss-crossing and interconnected tracks; within the pine forests it can all look the same. To add to the navigation issues, some of the forest roads used to the south are not yet on OS maps. Saying that, once on the ground you really can't miss them as they are pretty large scars through the forest.

It is owned by Danish retail billionaire Anders Povlsen, who has conservation-based intentions and is currently believed to be the largest landowner in Scotland. The rewilding work started around a decade ago and it is refreshing to see the results already – it is allowing the landscape to return to a more natural state with self-seeding native trees dotting the hills. It is a shift in mindset from the standard Highland estate management, but such a huge area of land in private hands has proved to be controversial, with questions on whether land tax or caps should be introduced. Whatever the motivations for Povlsen, it is positive to see this rewilding and it's a living experiment of what can be done when the number of deer and grazing sheep are greatly reduced.

As you ride through the regenerating land you might be lucky to hear or see signs of wildlife such as the turkey-like capercaillie, wild cats, pine martens, red squirrels and, in the skies above, various owls at dusk, ospreys and golden eagles through to the smaller crested tits. However, commercial forestry still rears its monotonous head even here. The ride takes in some huge, new forest tracks that seem to rather undermine some of the area's sensitivity and careful management; any objections to bike access pale in comparison to the changes to the landscape demanded by forestry. On the flip side, these new tracks are superb on a gravel bike.

Route overview

The ride is varied in the surfaces it uses; of particular note is one techy and boggy path section to the south of Loch an Eilein. This involves about 100 metres off the bike but it is all stop-start and will take some skill to ride on drop bars; the challenge is fun but

1 GLEN FESHIE GRAVEL. **2** THE PAVED ROAD UP GLEN FESHIE IS SCENIC ENOUGH TO RIVAL THE GRAVEL.

might not suit those from a road background or those new to the sport. The loop can be easily shortened to remove this lovely but techy section and the busy lochside trail too.

The ride through Glen Feshie uses a longer stretch of dirt and gravel singletrack but this is more mellow and, except for a river crossing and a short sharp climb, is all very drop-bar-friendly. The bridge over the Feshie has a wonderful wild swimming spot – the current under the bridge is strong, but there is a pool to jump into just past it. The bridge also has a sign saying it is the last crossing since the one up the glen was washed away.

To avoid sensitive landscapes this route doesn't use a few other optional singletrack sections and sticks to more paved roads or tracks. There are some optional fords, but all have alternative bridges too.

The climb up towards Coire Chrìon-alltain before Glen Feshie is steep with hairpins; it is on a new track that isn't yet on the OS map (it is marked as a small path through the forest). Instead, you'll find a smooth, wide, new forest track cut for logging. Obviously, watch for forestry work and logging trucks. The descent down to Glen Feshie is super-steep with distracting views over to Sgòr Gaoith and other neighbouring Munros of the Cairngorm plateau.

The track alongside the river is now a tarmac private road but it is a lovely ride and you rarely meet cars. You may hear the capercaillie along here too in spring. In late August the heather is in full bloom and the forests are loaded with blaeberries, red cowberries and midges. It is, however, well worth a trip at this time of year to see the area at its most beautiful.

Facilities and refreshments
The route is remote with few options for food and drink. However, a short detour at Feshiebridge takes you past Loch Insh to Kincraig and the wonderful **Old Post Office Cafe Gallery** – it's well worth a stop for a coffee and cake. On the road out of Feshiebridge there is sometimes a cake stall honesty box – the chocolate orange brownie is recommended. The start is in the car park at Loch an Eilein – towards the loch there is a small building selling drinks and ice creams over the summer.

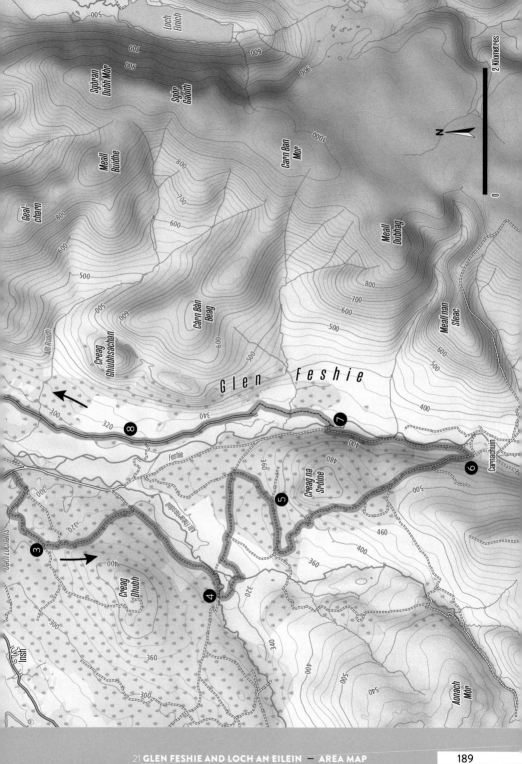

Loch
Einich

2 Kilometres

Sgoran
Dubh Mòr

Sgòr
Gaoith

N

Meall
Buidhe

Càrn Ban
Mòr

Geal-
charn

Meall
Dubhag

Meall nan
Sleac

Càrn Ban
Beag

Allt Ruadh

Creag
Chiuhsachan

G l e n   F e s h i e

⑧

⑦

Feshie

Allt Fhearnagan

Creag na
Sròine

⑤

⑥
Carnachuin

③

Sviunn Lochan

Creag
Dhubh

④

Inshi

Aonach
Mòr

1 THE NEW TRACK EXTENDING CLOSER TOWARDS LOCH GAMHNA. 2 THE RUINED CASTLE ON LOCH AN EILEIN.

Bike shops

Wee Bike Hub (T: 01528 544 751) and **Bothy Bikes** (T: 01479 810 111) in Kingussie or **Aviemore Bikes** (T: 01479 810 478) and **Alpine Bikes** (T: 01479 788 840) within in the large Tiso outdoor store in Aviemore all offer repairs and spares.

Public transport and access

This route is perfect for train travel with train stations at Aviemore and Kingussie on the main line to Inverness. However, at the time of writing, space for bikes has to be booked and is limited to two on most trains. At the car park at Loch an Eilein charges are per person, so it can be expensive for a full car – the car park usually has plenty of space and has ice creams for sale and toilets.

The route

🅢 Starting from Loch an Eilein car park, ride back along the access road and turn left on to the B970. As you ride south you pass an obvious track heading back up to the loch – this track has a locked deer gate, so stay on the road. Cross the River Feshie at Feshiebridge. (Here you can continue on to Kincraig via Loch Insh to visit the Old Post Office Cafe Gallery.)

❷ Just after Feshiebridge turn left on to a track with a green gate next to a house. The gravel track cuts across the forest to meet a paved road which runs up the western side of the River Feshie. Before you reach the Feshie, take a detour towards the pretty Uath Lochans.

❸ A left-hand turn takes you along a truly spectacular track across the flat grassland with epic views; later you head past a small building marked on OS maps as Corarnstilbeg.

❹ Cross a small footbridge over the Allt Chomhraig; this is signposted to *Braemar*. On the other side you are on a nice smooth gravel track; cross another footbridge (or ford the river) before heading uphill into a pine forest.

❺ This area has a lot of new tracks, so navigation using an OS map gets tricky. This is, however, the best part of the ride – the climb is big but well worth the effort.

GRAVEL RIDES SCOTLAND

THE SOMETIMES BUSY TRACK AROUND LOCH AN EILEIN.

6 Watch your speed as you're heading down to the River Feshie; it is steep with big panoramic views. Turn left on to a tarmac road heading north along the Feshie.

7 Cross a bridge over the Feshie (a sign facing the opposite way tells you this is the last crossing of the Feshie, since the bridge further upstream washed out). The singletrack on the other side is all pretty smooth; a river crossing near Achleum can mean wet feet, but it is unlikely to be a problem unless the river is in full spate.

8 The road north through Glen Feshie is a quiet tarmac road; you'll pass the Cairngorm Gliding Club.

9 Shortly after this, look out for the track to the right; there are no signposts but it is an obvious gravel track. This track then connects through to a narrower track and then a rough path which takes you to Loch Gamhna. There are two (approximately 1km) singletrack options here: the one shown on the map and in the GPX file (around the western shore of Loch Gamhna) is shorter but requires more hike-a-bike, while the other (which ends on the eastern shore of Loch Gamhna) is longer and has more techy riding, but a skilled rider in the dry could ride almost all of it on gravel bike. Either way, be aware that this is really mountain bike terrain and involves some techy root riding. You return to the Loch an Eilein circular track and you can opt for a short section or the full loop, depending on how busy it is. If this isn't for you, stay on the main track and follow the road back.

Other routes or attractions in the area
The route can be extended to the north, south or to the west towards Kingussie; the most obvious option is to combine with **22 Loch Morlich, Glenmore and Abernethy Forest** (pages 193–199) or carry on and attempt The Cairngorms Loop around to Braemar via Tomintoul. The route can be shortened easily by missing out the northern loop to Loch an Eilein and starting in the area around the village of Feshiebridge.

22 LOCH MORLICH, GLENMORE AND ABERNETHY FOREST

31KM/19 MILES

Introduction

This short route involves riding on great gravel through atmospheric pine forests before breaking out into spectacular views from the Ryvoan Pass. You really can't beat exploring peaceful forest tracks like these, especially in August with a carpet of purple heather and ripe blaeberrys and the soft sounds of wildlife everywhere around you.

The local area

This route is all about the spectacular natural environment. It takes in tracks around the RSPB's Abernethy National Nature Reserve at Loch Garten; the land over Ryvoan Pass is also managed by the RSPB. You might see capercaillie, black grouse, osprey, red crossbills and crested tits, among others. During a ride I witnessed three capercaillie fighting near Ryvoan – it was quite a sight.

The pine forests really make this area special; they create a haven for wildlife too. Abernethy Forest has endless back roads, lochans and paths to keep you riding longer and further than what is included here.

Ryvoan Bothy is a famous and well used shelter within Abernethy National Nature Reserve; it has a history as a crofters' house and is now maintained by the Mountain Bothies Association. It is rare to have the place to yourself given its accessible location. As you head down to Loch Morlich you pass Glenmore Lodge, Scotland's premier outdoor education and training facility – it's a great place to top up your skills or get that leader qualification you always wanted.

OPPOSITE THE START OF A BIKEPACKING TRIP HEADING TO RYVOAN PASS FROM THE EAST.

DISTANCE **31km/19 miles** — ASCENT **259m/850ft** — OFF-ROAD **80%**
START/FINISH **Loch Morlich** — START/FINISH GRID REF **NH 959096**
SATNAV **PH22 1QY** — GPS **57.1654, -3.7230** — MAP **OS Landranger 36, Grantown & Aviemore (1:50,000)**

GRAVEL SCALE
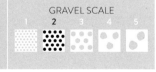

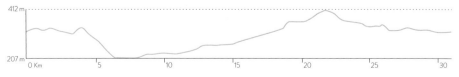

GRAVEL RIDES SCOTLAND

Aviemore is the real outdoor gateway hub of this area and a popular place for tourists; as a result, some hotspots get very busy in summer, but away from the lochs you'll usually be able to leave the crowds behind.

Route overview

The Ryvoan Pass is part of a classic mountain bike loop, but this variation is pretty much all gravel-bike-friendly. The descent from Ryvoan Pass is bumpy with a cobble-like construction, meaning it is rideable but vibrates your teeth out in places. After the bothy there are two steeper, rougher sections where most riders will opt to walk. Then it is all smooth tracks or roads back to the start. The path around Loch Morlich can be busy, so either avoid it by staying on the road or go slow at busy times. There are also countless variations on the exact route around the loch; almost all are drop-bar-friendly.

The section of private road after the B970 is loose in places and feels like gravel; however, where it passes a marshland it is so flooded it needs a detour on to a wooden boardwalk. On calm days in late summer this area can be brutal for midges, so pack some Smidge. In general, this route is a nice quick blast on good surfaces with no large climbs.

Navigation

The loop is best ridden clockwise to enjoy the descent back down from Ryvoan Pass to Glenmore. The route is easy to navigate in the most part, but the forests towards Nethy Bridge in the northern section of the route become a rabbit warren of roads, paths and tracks, so take a good map and GPS device. The start point is at Loch Morlich; at busy times if you're driving you may prefer to park towards Nethy Bridge to avoid the lochside crowds.

Facilities and refreshments

There are two or three options along the shores of Loch Morlich for cafes and ice creams, with the **Boathouse Cafe** near the large campsite being the pick. Towards Aviemore there are more options for a post-ride stop including **The Barn** on the Rothiemurchus estate.

OPPOSITE THE SMOOTH TRACK HEADING UP TO THE RYVOAN PASS FROM THE WEST; IT DOES GET MUCH ROUGHER!

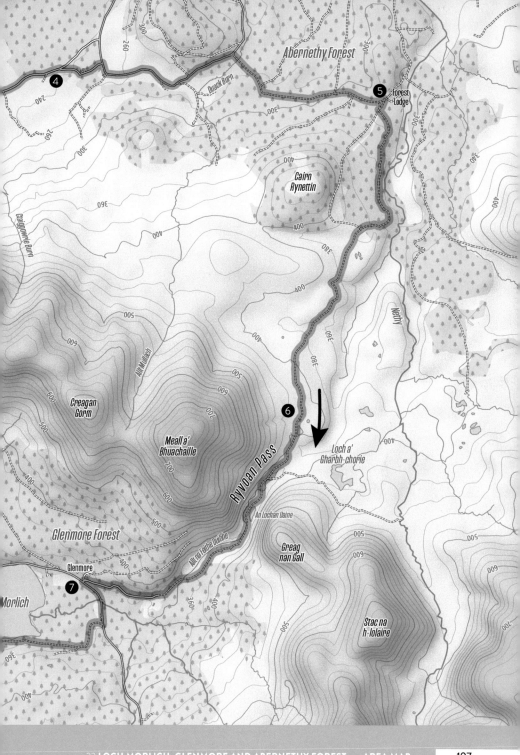

A PATH THROUGH THE TREES IN ABERNETHY FOREST.

Bike shops
Aviemore Bikes (T: 01479 810 478), **Alpine Bikes** (T: 01479 788 840) within in the large Tiso outdoor store in Aviemore and **Ride Scotland** (T: 01479 831 729) in Boat of Garten all offer repairs and spares.

Public transport and access
Aviemore railway station is close to the route (follow the Old Logging Way cycle path to reach Loch Morlich); Boat of Garten railway station is also a good option. The easiest access point by car to the route is at Loch Morlich, where there is a pay and display car park.

The route

S Starting from the shores of Loch Morlich head north-west on the Old Logging Way, a waymarked cycle path between Glenmore and Aviemore. Our route turns left off the main track on to a path; after 500m turn right off the path, following a sign to *Badaguish*.

2 Badaguish is an outdoor centre; keep left to avoid it and follow the lovely remote track out to the B970.

3 Turn right on to the B970 then turn right on to a track. The surface here varies between gravel and a paved, narrow road; halfway along it is permanently flooded and quite deep; a wooden boardwalk detour is required to pass.

4 A couple of right turns take you past some lovely houses nestled in the pine woods before you reach the RSPB's Abernethy National Nature Reserve and a gravel track to Forest Lodge. This track runs through uniform pine forest and is full of small birds and great riding.

THE ACCESSIBLE AND OFTEN CROWDED RYVOAN BOTHY IN THE RSPB RESERVE.

5 Just before Forest Lodge, turn right on to the Ryvoan Pass track. This is steep and rough in places, but fine on a gravel bike. The track passes through young pine trees before breaking out into the open at the high point with views of the mountains.

6 The descent to Glenmore starts and you soon pass Ryvoan Bothy; this accessible bothy is often busy overnight, but it is a nice place to shelter if the weather is coming in. You pass the pretty An Lochan Uaine before Glenmore where you reach the road by the Cairngorm Reindeer Centre.

7 Turn left to complete a loop of the stunning Loch Morlich on tracks and well-surfaced paths to get back to the start.

Other routes or attractions in the area

There are so many tracks around Nethy Bridge you could explore for days. However, the train also opens up the option of a linear ride: consider using Boat of Garten railway station to start and follow a winding route south ending at Kingussie. For a longer route, consider riding to Dalwhinnie or even take the Gaick Pass and end at Blair Atholl.

A MOODY GLEN AFFRIC – ONE OF SCOTLAND'S FINEST GLENS (ROUTE 26).

NORTH WEST SCOTLAND

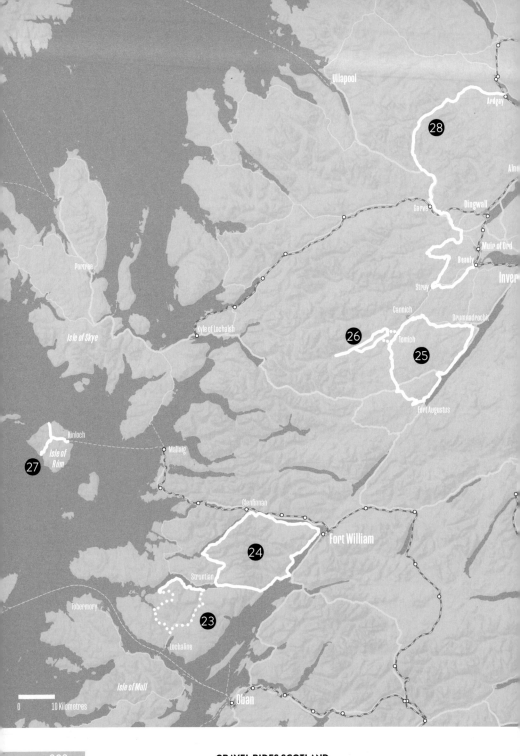

NORTH WEST SCOTLAND

This part of Scotland is rugged, rocky and not short on drama. While the gravel riding does tend to be rougher up here as it is so exposed to the elements, there is some fantastic gravel riding and it thoroughly deserves to be one of the areas included in this book. The weather dominates riding here; be it a feeling of hygge while sheltering from a lashing storm in a bothy or soaking up the scenery with wall-to-wall sunshine and feeling like you've won the lottery. The weather often passes through quickly, so it really is true that if it is raining, wait five minutes and you'll see the sun. Ensure that you're prepared for almost any weather whatever the time of year, especially if up high.

The main tourist town is Fort William, and Lochaber describes itself as the Outdoor Capital of the UK. For those that haven't visited in a while, the town is looking better than ever with new cafes and shops popping up. Ben Nevis, the highest peak in the UK, still dominates hikers' itineraries and the surrounding skyline.

West of Fort William lie remote peninsulas that receive fewer visitors: Arisaig, Moidart, Ardnamurchan and Morvern are all linked together by twisting single-track roads and a few nice gravel sections.

We can't overlook the *Harry Potter* viaduct at Glenfinnan, now probably as high on most visitors' bucket lists as the mountains. Booking a steam train ride out to Mallaig is a great option to keep kids and family happy while you sneak out for a gravel ride, or this train line opens up longer rides over towards the Isle of Skye, despite there being few gravel options on the island itself.

23 MORVERN PENINSULA
35KM/22 MILES

Introduction

A truly remote jaunt on an out-and-back through a forest along the shores of Loch Sunart, a Marine Protected Area. The optional full loop adds contrast with a steep climb in a mountain environment reminiscent of Iceland, but with more wildlife and eagles in the sky above.

The local area

Morvern is a remote peninsula bounded by the Ardnamurchan peninsula to the north, with its famous beaches; this forested coastline along Loch Sunart and south to the Sound of Mull is often overlooked. To get here you'll probably use a ferry, which is baffling when it isn't an island but certainly adds to the experience.

The area along Loch Sunart is a Marine Protected Area with otters, deer and other fauna abundant; the land is covered in weather-withered birch forest, all carpeted in mythical amounts of lichen and moss, before rolling directly on to the rocky foreshore. The beaches are littered with more shells than you'll have ever seen – this is both a delight and a reminder that most of our beaches are unprotected and subsequently support a lot less marine life. Sea eagles and golden eagles are often seen from the route as it heads inland, so keep your eyes to the skies whenever it is safe to do so.

At the end of the loch sit the ruins of Glencripesdale House; Glencripesdale Estate was once a vast Highland estate which diminished over time, culminating in the large house being blown

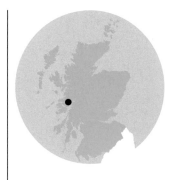

OPPOSITE THE REMARKABLE ROAD ALONGSIDE LOCH SUNART.

DISTANCE **35km/22 miles** — ASCENT **320m/1,050ft**
OFF-ROAD **100%** — START/FINISH Lay-by near Achleek, A884
START/FINISH GRID REF **NM 786597** — SATNAV **PA80 5XD**
GPS **56.6765, -5.6157** — MAP **OS Landranger 40, Mallaig & Glenfinnan; 49, Oban & East Mull (1:50,000)**

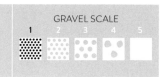

GRAVEL SCALE

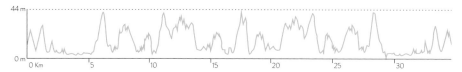

THE FUN FOREST ROADS ABOVE LOCH ARIENAS.

Navigation

The out-and-back option is pretty foolproof – the detour on to the shoreline is about as complicated as it gets. The full loop (**23a**) is a bit more challenging to navigate with two sections of plantation forest and various confusing junctions.

up by the army as a training exercise in the 1960s. The ruins do remain, but you'll need to look deep into the vegetation. Only the large Factor's house remains standing – it is in a lonely position surrounded by deer (and unfortunately lots of ticks).

There are some great options to extend this route for a bikepacking trip; most of these involve some road riding with a few obvious gravel sections. The area is perfect for wild camping by a remote beach overnight – just watch the weather and the large tidal range (don't camp on the beach) and you'll have a blast!

Route overview

To get the biggest issue clear from the start, the route extension (**23a**) is a brilliant ride but, at the time of writing, has locked 2.4-metre-tall deer gates in the forest past Glencripesdale. Therefore, it can't be fully recommended; however, the out-and-back route, on a good gravel track through woodlands along the shore of Loch Sunart, is still very rewarding, and worth riding on its own. Locked gates blocking responsible access are not allowed under the SOAC; it seems that the lack of visitors, rather than anything else, is the main explanation for not installing a pedestrian gate and there are a few stories of friendly interactions with the land manager. If you do want to ride **23a** then it is *not* suitable for heavy bikes (only one of the locked gates has a proper stile). (The full loop is shown on the map and has a GPX file –

VIEWS OF THE LOCH SUNART MARINE RESERVE.

23a Morvern peninsula: extension, distance: 65 kilometres, ascent: 1,122 metres, gravel rating: 3 out of 5, off-road: 60%.)

On the full loop, after clearing the gates there is a rewarding beast of a climb, taking you up into a remarkable Icelandic-esque landscape with craggy lines on the mountains, followed by a steep and loose descent. In the dry it can all be ridden with care and skill on drop bars in an anticlockwise direction, but most riders will prefer some short pushes on both the uphill and downhill sections. In a clockwise direction, you'll be pushing for a good chunk uphill, but the descent is smoother and more fun on a gravel bike.

The easiest place to start is near the small quay at Achleek. Be well prepared, as it is a long way to any facilities and there are only a handful of houses along the route. Hopefully you'll see more eagles than people.

The route uses some smooth and fast gravel forest roads to the west of Loch Arienas to reduce the amount of tarmac; however, an alternative is to just use the pleasant back road alongside Loch Arienas. In fact, the forest roads probably see as much traffic as the tarmac does, as commercial logging trucks use them to avoid the narrow single-track roads, so make your own choice as to which you prefer.

Facilities and refreshments
This is simple, as there are no facilities at all. There are some self-catering cottages, but the area is best described as remote.

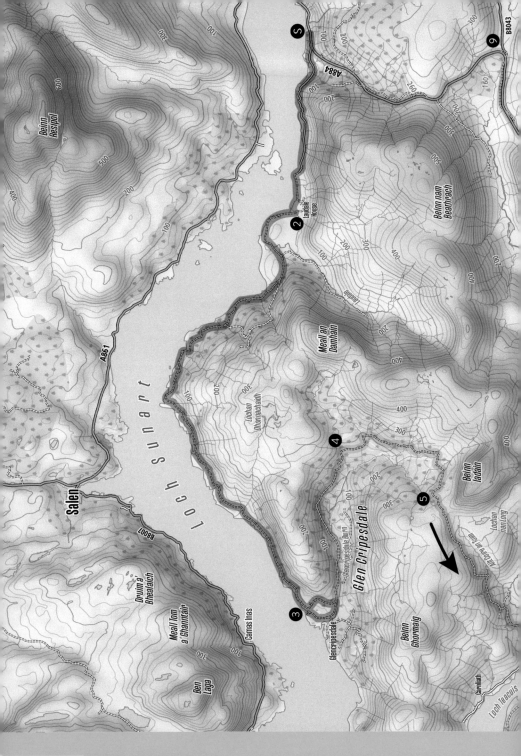

Beinn Resipol

600

500

400

200

100

A861

Loch Sunart

Salen

B8007

Druim a' Bhealaich

Meall Tom a' Ghamhrain

Ben Laga

300

100

300

Camas Inas

Glencripesdale

Glen Cripesdale

Glencripesdale Burn

Beinn Chaorach

Meall an Damhain

Lochan Vhannachraich

200

300

400

300

200

100

Laudale House

S

A884

B8043

300

100

100

200

260

300

400

500

200

160

Beinn nam Beathrach

Beinn Iadain

Lochan nan Long

Allt Doire an Lain

Gamhlach

Loch Teacuis

2

3

4

5

9

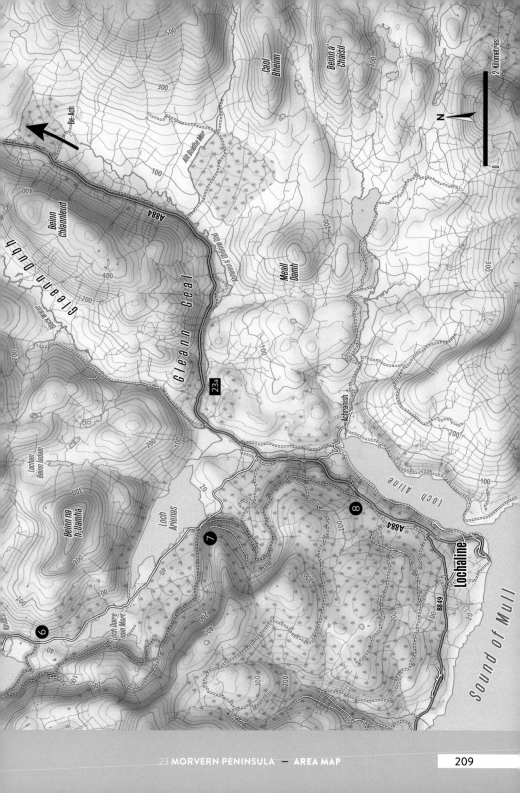

2 Kilometres

N

500

Caol Bheinn

Beinn a' Chaisil

300

Be-Ach

300

100

Allt Buidhe Mor

Abhainn a' Ghlinne Ghil

A884

Meall Damh

200

Beinn Chlaonleud

400

Gleann Dubh

200

200

Beck Water

300

200

Gleann Geal

100

22a

Achranich

200

100

100

Loch Aline

Lochan Beinn Iadain

200

100

20

Loch Arienas

8

7

A884

B849

Lochaline

Beinn na h-Uamha

300

300

Kiel Kol

200

40

Loch Doire nan Mart

40

200

400

200

300

300

200

6

100

200

Sound of Mull

20

1 THE START OF THE DESCENT TO LOCH TEACUIS. **2** THE BREATHTAKING VIEW OVER THE LOCH SUNART MARINE RESERVE.

Bike shops

The nearest bike shop is in Fort William, and therefore is of limited use for this route. Just in case, **Nevis Cycles** (T: 01397 705 555) is the best option.

Public transport and access

The Corran Ferry, which runs across Loch Linnhe to the south of Fort William, is the best access point. Be aware that the charges are higher for camper vans than for cars on the ferry. Many people will opt to park up and then get on the ferry with just their bike, but this adds quite a few miles. A few small lay-bys at Achleek provide some parking at the start of the route.

The easiest way to access this route on public transport is via train from Fort William, but it is some distance away.

The route

🅢 Starting from Achleek, head out along the track on the shore of Loch Sunart; the track is obvious and, while it undulates, it never strays far from the shore. Navigation should be easy.

2 After around 4km near Laudale House, there is a sign politely asking you to keep along the shoreline rather than going through the houses; this seems a fair request and the foreshore is almost all rideable. The track goes through stunning forest with loch-side views, passing some holiday houses.

3 The forest clears, and an old pier signals you are at Glencripesdale. Now it's decision time – explore the area and return the way you came or carry on for the full loop and expect to climb some tall deer gates. To complete the full loop (**23a**), head left into the forest just before the old pier at Glencripesdale. You'll probably see deer darting about and the area feels truly cut off and wild. The ride carries on along forest tracks climbing gently; navigation is quite straightforward, just don't cross the river. The first locked deer gate is fine and has a stile that should be manageable even with a loaded bike.

4 Follow the climb further up the hill through the forest. You next reach a gate with a wooden slatted panel, like a ladder, to aid climbing over. The track is shown as ending here on the latest OS mapping, but it doesn't end – it carries on and is correctly marked on OpenStreetMap. Next, you reach the third locked gate. This is around 2.4m high and doesn't have any helpful features to help you climb it – I managed it solo, but it was a real struggle. Be warned, especially for shorter

APPROACHING GLENCRIPESDALE ON THE STUNNING LOCHSIDE TRACK.

riders and heavier bikes. The good news is that the gates are now behind you, but the steeper section of climb begins. The forest thins as it curves uphill, and the track gets mossy and muddier in places as it rarely sees any use.

5 Finally, you reach the fourth locked gate where the track ends at the pass. To the left there is no fence so carry your bike around it. About 30m later the track carries on; presumably it has deliberately been stopped here to prevent vehicle access. Appreciate this absolutely stunning landscape as you look over to the Icelandic-looking Beinn Iadain and Bein na h-Uamha before you tackle the descent, which will rattle your eyes out of their sockets if you're not careful.

6 The easiest option is to follow the road back around to the start, or you can continue following 23a and head into the forest next to the end of Loch Teacuis. These forest tracks go up and down in parallel to the road but offer better views and they are on good gravel. You might see logging trucks, so ride aware.

7 The track brings you to the delightfully named Little Bonnet of Lorn on the shore of Loch Arienas. Join the next track on the right and head uphill.

8 After some amazing views, the track drops down to the A884 next to Loch Aline. Turn left (heading north) on the A884.

9 After about 15km keep left to stay on the A884 rather than joining the B8043. The fast descent back down to Achleek is fantastic fun.

Other routes or attractions in the area

This route is designed to link into **24 Loch Shiel, Glenfinnan and Loch Linnhe** (pages 213–219) for a bikepacking trip – take the train to Fort William and then the Camusnagaul Ferry to start this option. This route can also extend westwards to Drimnim: either do another loop of the lower Morvern peninsula, which requires a short hike, or catch the ferry over to Mull for a longer trip. Once on Mull, you can ride across the island and return to Oban. This makes a great linear ride when you start from Fort William railway station.

24 LOCH SHIEL, GLENFINNAN AND LOCH LINNHE
95KM/59 MILES

Introduction

A stunning lochside loop that uses undoubtedly one of the finest gravel tracks in Scotland; the single-track roads aren't bad either. At first glance this route has a lot of road riding – it is one of the few rides in this book with more road than gravel – but have faith and don't dismiss it until you've ridden it.

The local area

The riding is fast, fun and perfect for exploring on west coast gravel. The area is only a stone's throw from Fort William but feels so much more remote. In part this is because it usually requires travelling on a ferry to start the ride which only adds to the excitement.

Loch Shiel is a National Scenic Area with an abundance of birdlife. Key species include the protected black-throated diver and golden eagles; however, the area supports most of the birds of prey found in Scotland so keep your eyes to the sky. At the southern end of the loch lies Eilean Fhianain, one of the largest islands on the loch. It has a ruined medieval chapel, which is thought to have been built by Clan Ranald; unfortunately, it is just south of the route but you might still glimpse a sight of it.

At the northern end of Loch Shiel is the Glenfinnan Viaduct. Not only is it a stunning engineering feat with its 21 arches, which date back to 1901, but it's in the *Harry Potter* films too – just in case you're wondering why so many buses of foreign tourists are queuing alongside it.

OPPOSITE THE GREATEST GRAVEL RIDING IN SCOTLAND IS PROBABLY AT LOCH SHIEL.

DISTANCE **95km/59 miles** — ASCENT **748m/2,454ft** — OFF-ROAD **40%**
START/FINISH **Corran (western side of the Corran Ferry)**
START/FINISH GRID REF **NN 016637** — SATNAV **PH33 7AA**
GPS **56.7227, -5.2441** — MAP **OS Landranger 40, Mallaig & Glenfinnan; 41, Ben Nevis; 49, Oban & East Mull (1:50,000)**

GRAVEL SCALE

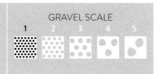

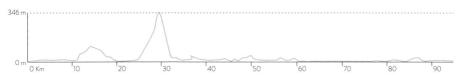

346 m

0 m

0 Km   10   20   30   40   50   60   70   80   90

GRAVEL RIDES SCOTLAND

Next to the viaduct is the Glenfinnan Monument; built in 1815, this 18-metre-high monument is a poignant reminder of the clansmen who gave their lives to the Jacobite cause. It is free to enter the site and for a fee you can climb to the top of the monument for a Highland panorama if your legs have the strength; more importantly, there is also a busy cafe on the site.

Route overview

At 95 kilometres this route is long, but it only has one significant climb and has the lowest technical grade in the book. The roads are quiet except for the short stint on the A830 at the northern end of Loch Shiel. It will be interesting if the ferry price hikes increase traffic on the narrow A861 along Loch Eil and Loch Linnhe.

Depending on the wind you can really fly along the loop; despite the rather epic distance it's certainly achievable in a long day. Other than the level of commitment to doing the whole 95-kilometre route, it would be a good ride for beginners.

Access to Glenfinnan requires following a footpath and footbridge on your left at the end of Loch Shiel; this helps to avoid a long detour on the A830.

Navigation

The route is written in a clockwise direction, but it really doesn't matter which way you choose. For such a long route navigation is pretty simple – just make sure you pick up the road heading south at Loch Eil. This is the A861, surely the narrowest A road in the UK. This is a long, committing route and once on the Loch Sheil gravel track it is a long way back to Corran.

Facilities and refreshments

The Inn at Ardgour and the **Nomad Cafe** are both in Corran at the start of the route. Further round the route is **Cafe Sunart** in Strontian and then **Monument View Cafe**, just off the route at Glenfinnan.

Bike shops

There are a couple of bike shops in Fort William – **Nevis Cycles** (T: 01397 705 555) is the best option.

OPPOSITE THE HARRY POTTER TRAIN HEADS OVER THE GLENFINNAN VIADUCT.

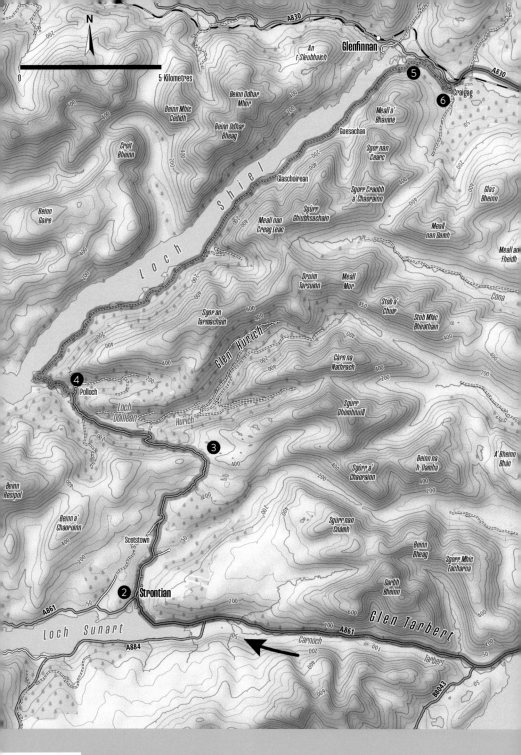

N

0 5 Kilometres

Glenfinnan

An t-Sleubhaich

⑤

Craigag

⑥

Beinn Odhar Mhor

Beinn Mhic Cedidh

Beinn Odhar Bheag

Meall a' Bhainne

Guesachan

Croit Bheinn

Sgor nan Cearc

Glaschoirean

Sgorr Creabh a' Chaorainn

Glas Bheinn

Meall nan Damh

Beinn Gaire

Loch   Shiel

Meall nan Creag Leac

Sgùrr Ghiubhsachain

Meall an Fheidh

Druim Tarsuinn

Meall Mor

Cona

Sgor an Tarmachain

Stob a' Chuir

Stob Mhic Bheathain

④

Polloch

Glen Hurich

Càrn na Nathrach

Loch Doilean

Hurich

Sgùrr Dhòmhnuill

③

A' Bheinn Bhàn

Beinn na h-Uamha

Beinn Resipol

Sgùrr a' Chaorainn

Beinn a' Chaoruinn

Scotstown

Sgùrr nan Cnàmh

Beinn Bheag

Sgorr Mhic Eacharna

Garbh Bheinn

Glen Tarbert

② Strontian

A861

Loch   Sunart

A884

Carnoch

A861

Tarbert

B8043

GRAVEL RIDES SCOTLAND

The route

S Head south on the A861. Once the ferry traffic has gone it is a quiet enough road; the locals do drive fast, though. The road runs along the shore of Loch Linnhe for 9km before a climb and descent over to Loch Sunart and Strontian.

2 From Strontian the only big climb of the ride begins; it is a bit of a beast as it zigzags up steep gradients, but the single-track road is peaceful and the views are well worth the effort.

3 A radio aerial that you can see for quite a way marks the top of the climb. A fun descent drops you down to Polloch.

4 In Polloch, follow signs to reach the car park. This is where the track starts and 22km of perfect gravel lies ahead. At first it passes through forest alongside Loch Shiel, then in the open with jaw-dropping mountain backdrops.

5 Finally, Glenfinnan Monument and Glenfinnan Viaduct are in view (on the left is a path to reach Glenfinnan village, if needed). A small climb takes you to the east and away. Turn left past a small walkers' car park and follow the track to reach the A830.

6 Turn right for a short stint on the A830 before turning right on to the A861. The A861 is certainly not a standard A road – it is a single-track road and it is simply a stunning section of riding regardless of whether you're on a gravel or road bike. You are never far from the shoreline and there are no real hills; it is usually quiet too.

7 Simply follow the A861 back to the ferry to complete an outstanding, smooth gravel ride.

Public transport and access

To get to the start of the route at Corran, take the Corran Ferry from Nether Lochaber. Leave your car at Nether Lochaber (there is a charge for car parking), as it is cheaper to go on the ferry as a foot passenger or as a cyclist than in a car. Also, be aware that the charges are higher for camper vans than for cars on the ferry.

The route is easy to get to via train – catch the train to Fort William and then take the Camusnagaul Ferry across Loch Linnhe to join the route. Alternatively, you could get the train to or park at Glenfinnan, and start the route there. On the northern section of the route, you can opt to get the train back to Fort William to save some energy (but probably not much time).

Other routes or attractions in the area

This route is designed to link into **23 Morvern peninsula** (pages 205–211), either as a loop or a linear ride. A great option for a longer linear ride is to start at Fort William railway station, ride part of this route (either the eastern or western section), link in with **23 Morvern peninsula**, catch the ferry over to Mull, ride across the island, then get the ferry to Oban, where there is a railway station.

OPPOSITE MORE VIEWS OF LOCH SHIEL.

25 FORT AUGUSTUS AND LOCH NESS
93KM/58 MILES

Introduction

This ride is perhaps the most epic in the book as it follows the toughest part of the Great Glen Way, then heads west up big climbs with long descents and even bigger panoramic views. While feasible as a day ride, it is more achievable as a bikepacking weekend – even two days would be good going for many riders.

The local area

Fort Augustus sits on the shores of Loch Ness; Nessie and tourists loom large here, the misty forests on its shores are enchanting places to explore. The fort which gives the village its name was built to quell any Jacobite uprisings, but it was captured in 1746. A line of forts was built along what is now the Caledonian Canal: the three most important were Fort George (in Inverness), Fort Augustus and Fort William. The village of Fort Augustus sits at a crossroads of military roads – to the east you can reach Ruthven Barracks near Kingussie via the Corrieyairack Pass, and to the west you can reach Glenelg, which is on the mainland opposite the Isle of Skye (our route makes use of part of this military road). Visitors to Fort Augustus can also enjoy the Clansman Centre where you can experience seventeenth-century clan life.

The landscape is vast and wild, but it has been industrialised to some extent. The plantation forest, tracks for a new line of pylons and countless wind farms dot the area; they are undoubtedly scars for the eyes but, as is a theme here, they have opened up some sublime gravel riding. The climb and descent

OPPOSITE VIEWS OVER LOCH NESS ON A BIKEPACKING ADVENTURE.

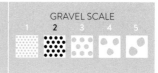

DISTANCE **93km/58 miles** — ASCENT **1,945m/6,381ft** — OFF-ROAD **70%**
START/FINISH **Fort Augustus** — START/FINISH GRID REF **NH 377097**
SATNAV **PH32 4BU** — GPS **57.1494, -4.6844** — MAP **OS Landranger 25, Glen Carron & Glen Affric; 26 Inverness & Loch Ness; 34, Fort Augustus (1:50,000)**

GRAVEL SCALE
1 2 3 4 5

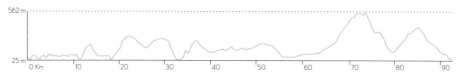

A CLASSIC SCOTTISH BACKDROP TO GRAVELLING.

Navigation

This is a long and wild route that needs experience to navigate. The first section follows the Great Glen Way as it heads north. This is waymarked but you need to make sure that you're on the low path and it is not always the easiest to follow. The forest tracks over to Glen Affric following the Affric Kintail Way are signposted. From Tomich heading south there's no marked route but it's straightforward once you're on the pylon track. The descent back to Fort Augustus is back in the forest but it is easy to stick on the main track.

heading south from Tomich is one of the most fun tracks in this book as it curves its way down across the open moorland like an MTB trail.

The first section of the route follows the Great Glen Way; this 121-kilometre route runs from Fort William to Inverness, passing lochs Lochy, Oich and Ness as well as the Caledonian Canal. It is all gravel-bike-friendly; the section near Fort William follows the canal towpath and is flat, while the northern section is more challenging.

The route also follows the Affric Kintail Way, a community-backed trail, mainly based on old drove roads, covering 71 kilometres from Drumnadrochit to Morvich. It gets progressively tougher as you head westwards; realistically, if doing the whole of the Affric Kintail Way you'll need a mountain bike to enjoy it properly (although the eastern section we use is gravel-bike-friendly).

Route overview

This long ride is ranked 2 out of 5 as it is mostly on smooth paths and tracks; however, the gravel is chunky in places and the Great Glen Way section is steep and rocky in parts.

Starting at Fort Augustus you follow mostly good gravel paths and tracks north on the Great Glen Way. This is waymarked; when descending be aware that the route is popular with walkers. It gives plenty of viewpoints across the placid waters of Loch Ness where exhausted cyclists have been known to see something in the water!

GRAVEL RIDES SCOTLAND

1 VIEWS ACROSS TO THE PINK HOUSE AT THE START OF THE CORRIEYAIRACK PASS. 2 WEATHER CLOSING IN AT ROUTE POINT 9.

The cyclists are so exhausted because the northern part of the Great Glen Way is not flat – it has some decent climbs and a few short and steep sections that will have you off the bike. However, on my last ride here a pine marten scurried across the path, so keep your eyes peeled in the forest too. The weather along the Great Glen often arrives with some speed – curtains of rain up the loch are followed by shafts of sunlight like searchlights seeking some lost fugitive. While dramatic, it is a reminder that you are on a committing and long route.

The section from Drumnadrochit heading west towards Cannich is all on good surfaces and follows the Affric Kintail Way, so watch out for the different signposts to follow through the forest. The first section out of town has a steep climb too. From Cannich you soon reach the pine forests at the start of Glen Affric and then the climb up on the pylon tracks towards Guisachan Forest. The track is a bit rough in the forest and your tired legs will curse it as the climb goes on forever – even after you leave the trees it's still uphill. However, after the high point on the pylon track the descent is superb, if a bit rough going at times.

The final section back to Fort Augustus is on more old military roads and, while the final climb looks bad when you see it across the glen, it isn't too bad riding it. The signposted Old Military Road mentioned in the directions is rough going – it is rideable but not ideal for gravel bikes, so you are better off staying on the main track as it hairpins down instead.

Facilities and refreshments

There are shops and cafes in Fort Augustus; you can also pick up that toy Nessie you always wanted. Invermoriston has a nice cafe called **Glen Rowan Cafe** on the A887. Drumnadrochit is a good-sized place with takeaways, cafes and shops; there is also Nessieland and the Loch Ness Centre for more souvenirs. After Drumnadrochit, there's nothing until you get back to Fort Augustus.

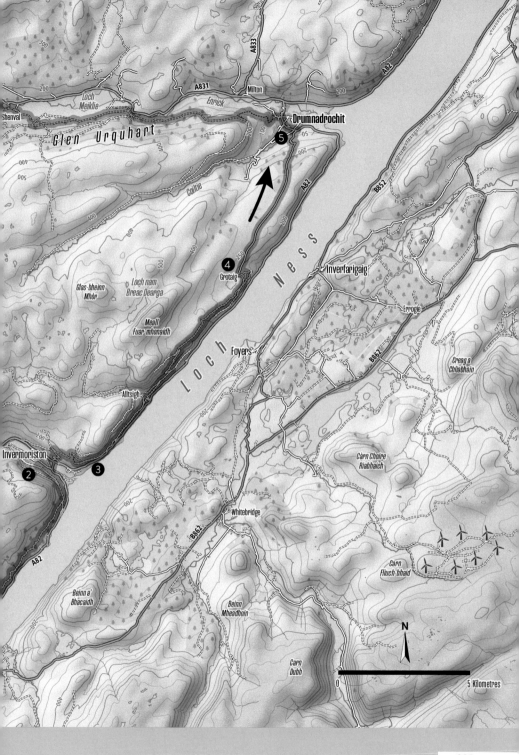

EXPLORING A DEAD-END OPTION JUST OFF THE ROUTE.

There are no dedicated bike shops in the area but the puntastic **Ness e'bikes** (T: 01320 366 864) at Girvans Hardware in Fort Augustus might be worth a call in an emergency.

Public transport and access

The nearest train stations are at Spean Bridge to the south or Inverness to the north. These are handy for a long linear ride, but no real help for this ride. Parking at Fort Augustus is easy (some is free, and some is pay and display). There is a small free car park next to the route starting point.

The route

S From Fort Augustus follow a *Great Glen Way* waymarker on a 10mph sign and head north. You want to follow the signs for the *low route*, as the high route is not gravel-bike-friendly. This means following a forest track parallel with the A82 as far as Invermoriston. This is a warm-up section with no big views of Nessie yet.

2 At Invermoriston cross over the bridge past some public toilets and on to a narrow back road that has a brutally steep set of hairpins. As this flattens a little at a gravel crossroads turn right, following a *Great Glen Way* waymarker. This next section is a bit frustrating as you follow the *low route* signposts. It descends down a steep path that is rocky in places and a bit muddy when wet – you effectively lose all that height immediately.

3 Back on a gravel track you undulate along the low path until the next tough climb up, giving you great views across the loch in both directions. The track stays high, so the views carry on when the trees allow.

4 Towards Drumnadrochit you climb up and join a tarmac road which our route follows into the town (the official Great Glen Way takes a slightly different path down into the town).

5 At Drumnadrochit, follow *Affric Kintail Way* signposts on to Pitkerrald Road. Keep following the signposts towards the village of Cannich (this section uses good forest tracks) until you join the A831.

GRAVEL RIDES SCOTLAND

A RUINED BOAT ON THE SHORES OF LOCH NESS (POSSIBLY CAUSED BY NESSIE).

6 The A831 isn't a great road; luckily there is a new section of the Affric Kintail Way that heads back into the forest after the hamlet of Millness. Rejoin the A831 for a short section alongside the River Glass near Cannich.

7 Just before the A831 crosses the River Glass, turn left (following a signpost for *Tomich*), leaving the Affric Kintail Way. Follow the minor road through Tomich.

8 Turn left into the forest at a green forestry signpost for the *Plodda Falls car park* (although you're not following the direction indicated by the signpost) – it is opposite Hilton Lodge on the OS map. This forest track is rough in places, but generally it is a nice steady climb up towards the powerlines just out of the forest.

9 Follow the powerlines down the outstanding gavel descent to Torgyle Bridge on the A887.

10 The track up and over to Fort Augustus is not on the 1:50,000 OS map, but it is on the 1:25,000. Don't follow the Old Military Road as this is very rough; follow the main track near the powerlines into the forest. Soon after, you'll spot another path signposted *Old Military Road*; this is rideable but rough so you're better off staying on the main track. Turn left on the tarmac road back into Fort Augustus.

Other routes or attractions in the area

This route is already a good distance, but the obvious extra option is to detour up Glen Affric (see **26 Glen Affric** (pages 229–235)) – an ideal option if you are looking to split the ride in two and fancy wild camping or staying in Glen Affric Youth Hostel. You can always incorporate this ride into a longer linear bikepacking ride from Inverness to Fort William, detouring around this loop before carrying on along the rest of the Great Glen Way. Remember that the Affric Kintail Way is more suited to mountain bikes, but you wouldn't be the first to ride it on drop bars – whether this is fun is strongly debatable!

26 **GLEN AFFRIC**
35KM/22 MILES

Introduction

Glen Affric is one of the classic Scottish glens with glistening lochs and surrounded by stunning mountains, but it is the natural Caledonian pine forest that sets it apart. This ride takes all this in on a fast, short blast.

The local area

Often described as the most beautiful glen in Scotland, Glen Affric is home to the third largest area of ancient Caledonian pinewood in Scotland. On a dry, sunny day, the waft of fresh pine as you ride along the tracks here is the ultimate immersion into the landscape. After the trees fade away the views get more and more impressive until you glimpse the iconic Five Sisters of Kintail in the west. The glen presents quite a few options for riding; admittedly, many that make nice loops are more suited to a mountain bike than a gravel bike. However, like the Linn of Dee over in the eastern Cairngorms, the scenery is well deserving of a mostly out-and-back ride.

With a standard Scottish history of an estate passing between various rich lairds, most of the land in Glen Affric was sold to the forestry commission in 1951; some of the land remains in private hands. The glen holds just about every possible protection, from a National Nature Reserve to a Site of Special Scientific Interest. The upper reaches of the glen are home to rewilding projects from both the National Trust for Scotland and Forestry and Land Scotland, the aim being to extend and connect wildlife corridors through this unique glen in each direction so the wildlife will only

OPPOSITE RIDING AT THE HEAD OF GLEN AFFRIC NEAR THE GLEN AFFRIC YOUTH HOSTEL.

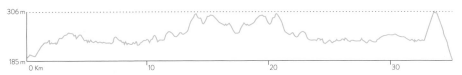

DISTANCE **35km/22 miles** — ASCENT **348m/1,142ft** — OFF-ROAD **70%**
START/FINISH **Dog Falls car park, Glen Affric** — START/FINISH GRID
REF **NH 283282** — SATNAV **IV4 7LY** — GPS **57.3120, -4.8524**
MAP **OS Landranger 25, Glen Carron & Glen Affric (1:50,000)**

GRAVEL SCALE

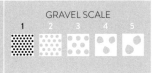

GRAVEL RIDES SCOTLAND

get better and better in the future. Look out for otters and red- and black-throated divers on the river, pine martens in the forests and ospreys and golden eagles in the skies.

Route overview

In terms of gravel riding, the best option is a loop of Loch Beinn a' Mheadhoin; there is a track and also some doubletrack all around Loch Affric too, but a quick glance on the OS map shows it marked as a path, which tells you it is rough going in places. In the dry, this doubletrack is fine for experienced gravel riders, but in all other conditions you're better off with fat tyres or missing it off.

This ride heads to the western end of Loch Affric and retraces its tyre marks back east to complete the loop of Loch Beinn a' Mheadhoin on a fun single-track paved road. If you fancy more miles you can detour up into the forest at the eastern end of the route for some fun, smooth gravel between the pines – **26a Glen Affric: extension** (distance: 41 kilometres, ascent: 529 metres) is shown on the map and has an accompanying GPX file.

You can carry on west to Glen Affric Youth Hostel, high up in the glen, but the track gets rougher and rougher as you get further along. The path beyond the youth hostel is no longer fun without suspension and soon after that all riders will be walking a lot. It's a shame as it would open up some interesting long-distance rides.

The best place to start the route is at Dog Falls – it's a popular spot for bikers and hikers. Dog Falls itself and even Badger Fall along the lower River Affric are worth a peek. Especially on a summer's day, as the river has plenty of tempting pools for a post-ride wild swim.

Navigation
This route is showcasing Glen Affric, so navigation is pretty simple. It's simply a loop of Loch Beinn a' Mheadhoin and then an out-and-back as far up Glen Affric as you fancy – you'd do well to get too lost on this route.

Facilities and refreshments
There are no services on this route (other than the kitchen in the Glen Affric Youth Hostel if you've booked an overnight stay). The area is perfect for responsible wild camping if you're doing a longer route in the area.

OPPOSITE IT'S VIEWS LIKE THIS THAT MAKE GLEN AFFRIC SO SPECIAL.

Loch Mullardoch

Toll
Creagach

Tom a'
Choinich

An Leth-
chreag

Stob a'Choire
Dhomhain

Sron
Gharbh

Gleann nam Fiadh

Abhainn Gleann
nam fiadh

Beinn a'
Mheadhoin

Am Meallan

Sgurr na
Lapaich

G l e n   A f f r i c

Loch Affric

Allt Garbh

Loch nan
Gillean

Athnamulloch

Càrn Glas
Iochdarach

N

0   2 Kilometres

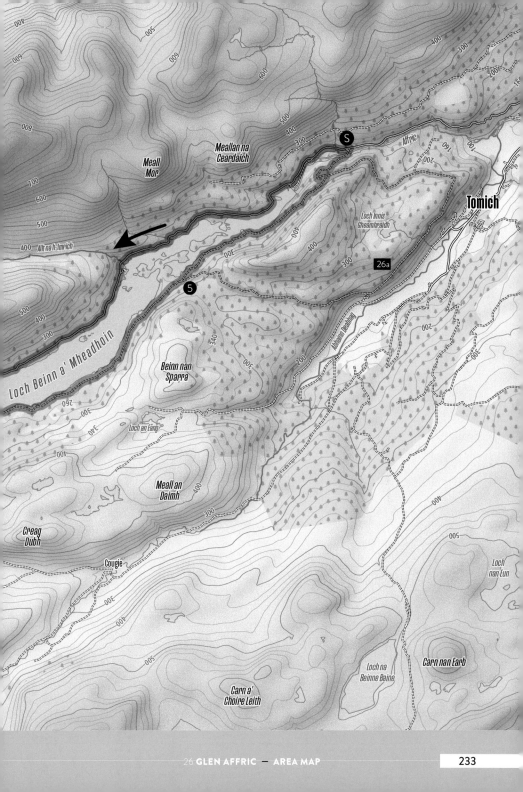

Meall Mór

Meallan na Ceardaich

S

Affric

Tomich

Loch Innis Gheamhraidh

Allt na h-Imrich

26a

Loch Beinn a' Mheadhoin

5

Beinn nan Sparra

Abhainn Deabhag

Loch an Eàng

Meall an Daimh

Creag Dubh

Cougie

Loch nan Eun

Carn a' Choire Leith

Loch na Beinne Baine

Carn nan Earb

GRAVEL RIDES SCOTLAND

The route

S From Dog Falls get the tarmac out of the way and head west along the road on the northern shore of Loch Beinn a' Mheadhoin. This undulating single-track road is a dead end and is easy to follow.

2 When the tarmac ends there is a small car park and a few walking paths, including one to a great viewpoint. Cross the river on the now gravel track. From here, the route is an out-and-back along the southern shore of Loch Affric on the Affric Kintail Way – a stunning ride on good quality gravel. You can go as far as you like as you'll return the same way.

3 At the head of Loch Affric, you can stroll down to the small sandy beach and admire a green roofed hut that has recently been built by the estate. It's a great spot for lunch. (You can continue heading west along the glen, but once over the bridge the track does start to deteriorate into larger rocks and steeper inclines. It is rideable by gravel bike as far as Glen Affric Youth Hostel, which makes a great overnight stop.) Head back the same way along the southern shore of Loch Affric.

4 Don't cross the bridge; stay on the gravel track on the southern side of Loch Beinn a' Mheadhoin instead. This good gravel track goes up and down and takes you into pine forests.

5 There are a couple of options here: either follow the Affric Kintail Way back to Dog Falls or follow **26a Glen Affric: extension**, adding about 6km of gravel to your ride. If you opt for the longer route, there's a fast descent towards Tomich; make sure you look out for a left turn soon after leaving the forest. This forest road loops back and takes you to the Affric Kintail Way and back to the start.

Bike shops

There are no dedicated bike shops in the area but the puntastic **Ness e'bikes** (T: 01320 366 864) at Girvans Hardware in Fort Augustus might be worth a call in an emergency.

Public transport and access

The nearest railway stations are at Spean Bridge to the south or Inverness to the north – ideal for a long point-to-point but no real help for this ride. The best place to start is Dog Falls car park (parking charge); it's a popular spot for bikers and hikers so spaces might be tight in high season.

Other routes or attractions in the area

The ride connects well with **25 Fort Augustus and Loch Ness** (pages 221–227). As mentioned, the path heading west from Glen Affric Youth Hostel is more suitable for a mountain bike rather than a gravel bike, so is best avoided. Likewise, don't be tempted by the path from the hostel south along An Caorann Mòr to the A87. It isn't even fun on a mountain bike – saving you from carrying a gravel bike up this boggy glen is worth the cost of this book alone!

OPPOSITE PERFECT LOCHSIDE GRAVEL AT LOCH AFFRIC.

27 ISLE OF RÙM
33KM/21 MILES

Introduction

This route might look a bit random for those that know the beautiful and dramatic small island of Rùm. Many will ask: 'Why is an island with no roads in the book?' Well, why not – there's no tarmac so every track on the island is gravel.

The local area

The small west coast island of Rùm is remote, wild and wonderful. The best way to see it is to take a gravel bike and ride all the tracks on the island – they total 33 kilometres but with a hearty 587 metres of ascent. Heck, this ride is so good why not do it every day you're on the island? Better still, combine it with some hiking.

The island is mostly owned by NatureScot after being bequeathed with the condition it is managed as a nature reserve. The Isle of Rùm Community Trust is very active on the island – it is possibly best known for their occasional national press features seeking families to relocate to 'live the dream' and croft on the island. Being a nature reserve, the island is home to an abundance of wildlife, some more wild than others, including red deer, white-tailed and golden eagles, various marine mammals, feral goats, ponies, Highland cattle and way more besides.

Once you leave the ferry and the area around Kinloch, it really does feel empty of any humans but, like much of the Highlands, this wasn't always the case. Almost all the residents were evicted during the Highland Clearances and headed off

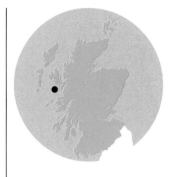

OPPOSITE THE TRACK TO HARRIS IS TRULY SPECTACULAR.

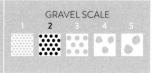

DISTANCE **33km/21 miles** — ASCENT **587m/1,926ft** — OFF-ROAD **100%**
START/FINISH **Rùm ferry slipway** — START/FINISH GRID REF **NM 412992**
SATNAV **PH43 4RR** — GPS **57.0111, -6.2646** — MAP **OS Landranger 39, Rùm, Eigg, Muck & Canna (1:50,000)**

GRAVEL SCALE

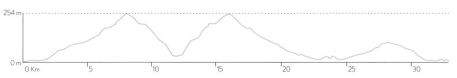

RÙM HAS DRAMA IN ABUNDANCE, ESPECIALLY WITH A LITTLE SNOW ON THE TOPS.

Navigation

If you get lost here with two tracks and one junction on the entire island, then the rest of the book is going to prove to be hard work! Make sure you bring a map though, as it's helpful for exploring hidden corners on foot too.

Facilities and refreshments

The island has a good variety of quirky accommodation. The main campsite is inexpensive and very pleasant; there is a recently opened bunkhouse, a B&B and some glamping pods too. Further afield, there are two bothies maintained by the Mountain Bothies Association (the bothies are not accessible by bike; they both can get busy) and some wild camping potential too, although it is strongly recommended to use the island accommodation to support the community if you can. There is a cafe that opens seasonally in the village hall, a post office and a small but well-stocked shop.

to Nova Scotia in the 1820s. The population decreased from 450 residents to around 50 by the end of the nineteenth century. The population was initially replaced by sheep; later, red deer were introduced for shooting.

The fascinating story of Rùm really steps up in 1888 when the island was bought by the Bullough family, who were Lancashire mill owners. The Bulloughs were ridiculously rich and, after purchasing the island, they built Kinloch Castle; if it is open when you visit, a tour of the castle it is well worth it. In its prime, the place was absolutely bonkers – there were the usual collections of fancy sculptures and artwork, but there were also squash courts and palm trees, alligators lived in a glasshouse and it was one of the first private residences in Scotland to have electricity. It even had air conditioning in the billiards room. All of this was transported to this remote Scottish island for occasional high society events. The future of the castle is currently in doubt – the restoration costs are exorbitant and most commercial uses of the castle would not be appropriate given its remote location within such an important nature reserve.

Rùm was essentially shut for generations – members of the public were discouraged from visiting – and it became known as the forbidden island. Only in 2005 with the introduction of the SOAC did the island fully reopen.

Route overview

Now you understand a bit more about why the island is so unique, how about the gravel riding? The riding is all drop-bar friendly and on relatively well-used 4x4 tracks; while it isn't all silky smooth, there are no big surprises for gravel riders.

1 MAKING FRIENDS WITH THE *COOS*. 2 ANOTHER ANGLE ON THE TRACK TO HARRIS.

On the track towards the centre of the island, a small steady climb gets you high up enough to ensure a panoramic view to the bay, with the Skye Cuillin as a ridiculously beautiful backdrop. The route first goes south on a track towards Harris – a steady climb takes you up to around 250 metres in height and offers a great perspective over the island and the Rùm Cuillin mountains. After a short descent, dodging photogenic Highland cows and Rùm ponies, you reach Harris, a small, isolated bay dominated by the Bullough Mausoleum. This building looks like a Greek temple picked up and plonked in possibly the least expected location. It really is a special spot; you can ditch the bike and climb nearby peaks from this point if you want to see more of the island. Return to the centre of the island then take the second track north to the beautiful lonely sandy beach at Kilmory, before returning to the ferry.

The midges can be overbearing on calm days – potentially a ploy to get you to book one of the indoor accommodation options on the island. The ferry can be easily affected by bad weather, as it crosses relatively open seas en route to the island.

The route

S Ride west from the ferry and turn left to reach Harris.

2 Retrace your route to the junction in the centre of the island; turn left to reach Kilmory.

3 Return to the ferry via the junction in the centre of the island.

Bike shops
None in the local area.

Public transport and access
The route starts at the ferry slipway; while it should be obvious, there are no cars allowed on the island without a permit and there really is no need for a car. Rùm is refreshing as it forces you to travel either on foot or bike. Getting here is easier than you might think with the ferry leaving from Mallaig, west of Fort William. The ferry takes a route around the other Small Isles so, depending on the schedule, one way will take longer than the other. Keep your eyes peeled for whales and dolphins in the sea and white-tailed eagles in the sky.

Other routes or attractions in the area
All add-ons require a ferry.

Sound of Canna

Kilmory Bay

Kilmory **3**

Kilmory Glen

Kilmory

Loch Sgaorishal

Sgaorishal

Loch Beauty

Glen Shellesder

Guirdil

Bloodstone Hill

Minishal

Isle of Rùm

Sròn an t-Saighdeir

Orval

Àrd Nev

Long Loch

Àrd Mheall

Loch an Dornabac

An Dornabac

Glen Dulan

Harris **2**

Abhainn Rangail

Glen Harris

N

0   2 Kilometres

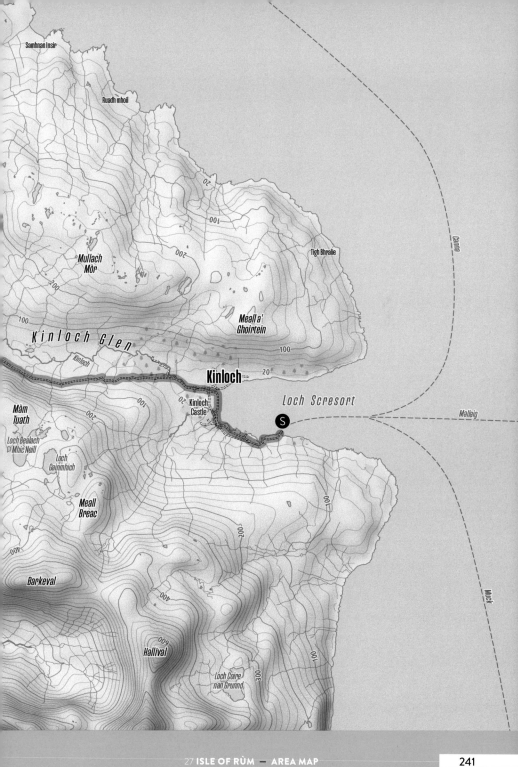

28 BEAULY TO ARDGAY
120KM/75 MILES

Introduction

A superb, proper gravel route, riding between two train stations – this is an adventure into some big, open, northern scenery. The route passes Orrin Reservoir and Loch Vaich, in between some classic whaleback mountains, all on superb gravel tracks or quiet back roads, with some very short stretches on main roads.

The local area

The area around Beauly is a great start to the route; it was apparently named by Mary Queen of Scots when she visited in 1564 and commented: '*Ç'est un beau lieu*' (what a beautiful place). If nothing else, it is proof that every corner of Scotland seems to have its own Mary Queen of Scots story.

The hydro dam at Glen Orrin is gigantic – a huge brutalist concrete structure spanning two openings across the glen. Completed in 1961, it certainly reflects the architecture of the time. The vast concrete also gave Scottish bikepacking one of its most iconic overnight stops – the Hydro Bothy, originally an old cement store, was a bare and basic bothy which was notorious with bikepackers passing through the area. Sadly, it has recently been demolished.

Lower Glen Orrin is a delight, especially where the river crashes through rapids that were originally part of planned grounds. It is now so wild feeling it is hard to tell this was the case; to the eastern side of the river the forest is planted with a remarkable array of fir and conifer trees, all now gigantic

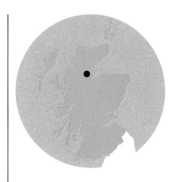

OPPOSITE THE ISOLATED AND WILD TRACK ALONGSIDE LOCH VAICH.

DISTANCE **120km/75 miles** ASCENT **1,133m/3,717ft** OFF-ROAD **60%**
START/FINISH **Beauly railway station/Ardgay railway station**
START/FINISH GRID REF **NH 520458/NH 600904**
SATNAV **IV4 7EZ/IV24 3DR** GPS **57.4782, -4.4699/57.8810, -4.3626**
MAP **OS Landranger 20, Beinn Dearg & Loch Broom; 21, Dornoch & Alness; 26, Inverness & Loch Ness (1:50,000)**

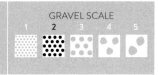

GRAVEL SCALE
1 2 3 4 5

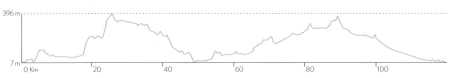

STARTING THE DESCENT DOWN TOWARDS THE CRAIGS.

Navigation

The direction ridden will be mostly dependent on your logistical arrangements; however, the prevailing wind is from the south-west so starting at Beauly and riding north makes most sense from that point of view.

The route itself is relatively easy to navigate for such an epic ride; the remote tracks are pretty clear once you are on them. The trickiest parts to navigate are from Beauly to the track to Orrin Reservoir and between Glen Orrin and the turn off towards Loch Vaich. This involves a series of forest tracks to avoid the fast A835.

specimens towering into the sky. This classic Victorian estate design wouldn't be out of place in a botanic garden.

From Glen Orrin the route passes north through Contin, home of the infamous Strathpuffer – a 24-hour mountain bike race held in winter. For those familiar with the event and the area in winter, rest assured it looks very different in the height of summer, with the dark and snow replaced by meadows and wildflowers.

Little Garve Bridge near Ben Wyvis is an old military road bridge that also has a nice wild swimming spot. There is also the Wyvis Natural Play Park, which is signposted as you ride past – if you are here with kids this is a unique place for them to enjoy. The Ben Wyvis area is a special place and very popular with walkers – not just the many Munro baggers, also those who like to explore the nature reserve around its base and those who have a soft spot for this unique mountain. To the north-west of Ben Wyvis lies Loch Vaich. It is a lovely loch with a very natural feel, which is a nice surprise considering that it is artificial – the concrete dam enclosing the loch was built in 1957.

The Glencalvie Estate at the northern end of the route is seen as one of the best sporting estates in the Highlands, boasting the clean, clear waters of the River Carron and hills full of red, roe and sika deer. For those with deep pockets, the spectacularly located Glencalvie Lodge can be rented.

THE SECOND DAM CROSSING AT ORRIN RESERVOIR.

Route overview

The far north of Scotland has some epic wild gravel tracks; however, the distance to get here and the sparseness between loops means the area is generally better suited to point-to-point rides. This route is the most northerly in the book and passes through spectacular, wide-open spaces.

Realistically, this is an overnight adventure, whether from the distance or the logistics of getting the train here; however, it is tempting to try it as a one-day challenge ride in midsummer. It is far enough north that in midsummer you'll not need lights, for a late finish or an early morning.

The ride follows a few back roads, but it is based around two long stretches of fantastic, well-surfaced and isolated gravel tracks. The first is to Orrin Reservoir and Glen Orrin – this is a classic Scottish gravel loop, but, as part of a linear ride, the fun keeps coming with the second stretch on an epic track past Loch Vaich up to Glencalvie. All the gravel is well maintained despite its remoteness; there are few surprises along the way.

It should go without saying, but be aware that this area is very sparsely inhabited and gets few visitors outside of peak season, so be prepared and self-sufficient when exploring this route.

Facilities and refreshments

Beauly has shops and a few takeaway options. Outside of Beauly the options are limited; **Contin Village Store** has a sign proudly proclaiming it as the last shop until Ullapool or Inverness. On the short section on the A835 south of Loch Vaich, the **Inchbae Lodge Inn** serves food when open.

There's some accommodation in Ardgay, including some glamping pods, to help get an early start on the route if riding north to south.

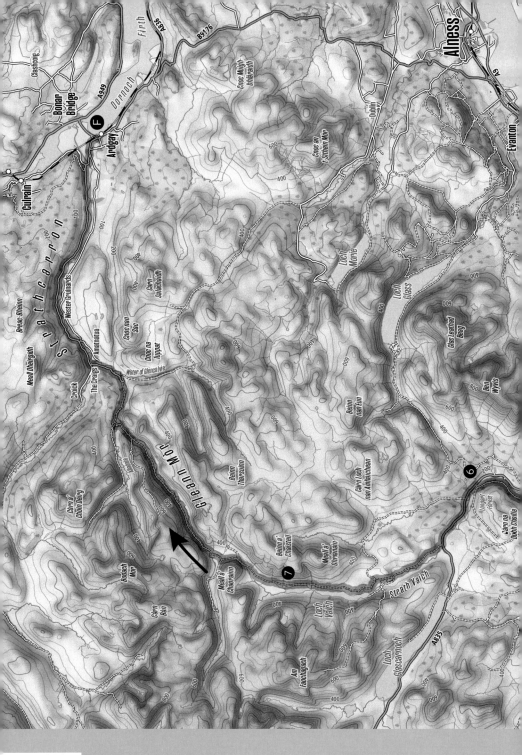

THE TRULY WILD MOORLAND CROSSING TOWARDS ORRIN RESERVOIR.

Bike shops
OrangeFox Bikes (T: 01463 870 346) is north of Beauly near Muir of Ord. Just off-route north-east of Contin is **Square Wheels** (T: 01997 421 000), while **Heaven Bikes** (T: 07543 466 699) is randomly in a post office in Bonar Bridge, just north of Ardgay.

Public transport and access
This route is all about using the trains. The route direction will no doubt be determined by your ride logistics: train times and whether you drive or catch the train to start the route. The trains do run reasonably early so, if parking at one end of the route, you can get a good start and then take your time.

The route

S Starting at Beauly railway station, head south-west past a large (dusty) quarry for a short section on the A831 – this is the busiest road of the route so ride aware. After 2km turn left over Black Bridge with a hydro dam on your right. Just to the south (off-route) is Beaufort Castle. Continue on narrow back roads near the River Beauly.

2 Turn right over the River Glass on a narrow bridge to reach Struy. Then, after about 1.5km on the A831, the track to Orrin Reservoir begins.

3 The track can be wet at times after it leaves Lochan Fada, but it is generally a good gravel ride and is best described as lonely as it is way out in the moors.

4 Orrin Reservoir is a behemoth of 1960s concrete in an open glen with great views of the mountains, some to the west and south-west being Munros. The descent is on tarmac but is a lot of fun; take the north bank of the river for a great section past huge old-growth fir trees. Then there is some road riding north to reach Contin.

A STUNNING SUMMER'S DAY ALONG THE LOCH VAICH TRACK.

5 Contin has the last shop before the end of the route, so stock up if needed. The route then follows forest roads and back lanes, first on one side of Black Water, and then on the other. The gravel section opposite Ben Wyvis, in particular, is fantastic.

6 Finally, the gravel options end for a short section on the A835; it isn't a particularly nice road so get your head down and get it done fast. Turn right, heading north on to a single-track road towards Loch Vaich, keeping to the right of the river.

7 Follow this superb remote track, passing Loch Vaich. Eventually the track merges into a back road then detours on to the south side of the River Carron to reach Ardgay railway station.

Other routes or attractions in the area

There are two ways to make this ride even longer. One is to loop south from Glencalvie Lodge in Alladale and head south to Alness on epic gravel tracks. This leaves either a train ride back from Alness railway station or a ride all the way to Beauly via roads and cycle paths for an even longer road ride.

The other option is to keep heading north to Cape Wrath or John o' Groats on the Great North Trail, a route that Cycling UK put together which uses the same section of track past Loch Vaich as this route. ***www.cyclinguk.org/ offroadcampaigns/great-north-trail***

There is also a great loop around Ben Wyvis that is worth looking up too.

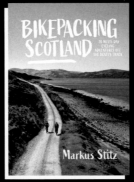
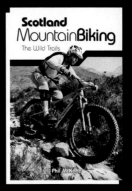

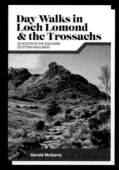

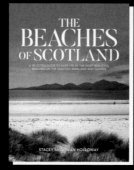

RIDING THE CORRIEYAIRACK PASS MILITARY ROAD.